The Power of Her Presence

A Tribute to the Everyday Strength and Lasting Influence of a Mother

I

Dedication

To the one who carried me before I ever knew my own strength…

To the woman whose heartbeat was my first rhythm…

To the mother who gave until there was nothing left to give—yet still found a way to give more…

This book is dedicated to **my mother**, who transitioned from this life on **June 29, 1992**, but whose presence remains woven into every day I live. Though I can no longer see her, I feel her with me—in my thoughts, my prayers, and the choices I make. I know in my heart that she is watching over my brother and me, and that she sees how her sacrifices, her faith, and her love were not in vain.

She was not loud, but she was powerful.

She didn't seek praise, but she shaped a legacy.

She may not have had much by the world's standards, but she gave us everything that truly matters—faith, strength, wisdom, and unconditional love.

This book is more than just a reflection of my gratitude.

It's a tribute. A thank you. A celebration.

It is a way of saying **"thank you"** to **all mothers**—those who are with us and those who have gone on. To every woman who has sacrificed quietly, loved deeply, prayed faithfully, and stood strong in the face of adversity… this book is for you.

Your presence, seen or unseen, continues to shape generations.

We honor you. We celebrate you. We thank you.

— With all my heart,

Your son. Your daughter. Your children.

Still rising because of your presence.

Ethan

About the Author

Ethan L. Ketterer is a devoted author, educator, speaker, and encourager whose life's mission is to uplift, empower, and remind others of their God-given purpose—especially in seasons when they may feel overlooked or undervalued.

He writes from a place of deep faith, personal reflection, and lived experience. His stories are marked by authenticity, encouragement, and spiritual insight. As the founder of the **KTURN brand**, Ethan has committed his life and work to helping others make "the right turn" in life—toward hope, healing, growth, and purpose.

He is the author of several impactful titles including:

- **A Seat at the Table** – A call for unity, collaboration, and mutual respect among stakeholders in education and beyond.
- **Access Granted** – A bold declaration that delays, denials, and detours do not have the final say over your destiny.

- **In the Driver's Seat** – A motivational reflection on taking ownership of one's life, decisions, and future.

Through his books, journals, speaking engagements, and the KTURN platform, Ethan empowers readers from all walks of life—educators, parents, students, faith communities, and everyday individuals—to live with clarity, confidence, and conviction.

KTURN's Commitment to You

At the heart of KTURN is a simple but powerful promise:

To provide motivation, inspiration, encouragement, and empowerment.

We're not just a brand—we're a movement. A family. A source of light when life feels dim, and a voice that reminds you of who you are and what you're capable of becoming.

Whether you're reading a book, attending a workshop, using one of our journals, or sipping from a KTURN mug—our message remains the same:

You matter. You're seen. And there's still more ahead for you.

Thank you for allowing us to journey with you.

Thank you for choosing to make a turn toward something greater.

With purpose,

Ethan L. Ketterer

Founder, KTURN

Introduction

The Power of Her Presence

There are some voices that live within us long after they go quiet. Some hands that stop reaching for us but still manage to hold us up. Some hearts that, even when no longer beating, pulse through everything we are. That is the power of a mother's presence.

This book is not just a tribute to my own mother—it's a tribute to *all* mothers. To the ones who are still with us and the ones we carry in our hearts. To the mothers who raised children in silence, with strength. Who held it all together when everything around them was falling apart. Who went unnoticed, unthanked, uncelebrated—yet never unloved.

We live in a world that often waits for one Sunday in May to honor mothers. But the truth is, if you had a mother who loved you, sacrificed for you, believed in you, or simply showed up for you—*one day* will never be enough. Not even close.

This book was written to fill in the space between those Mother's Days. The space where real honor lives—not in flowers or cards, but in gratitude. In how we live. In how we remember. In how we carry their legacy forward.

Whether you're reading this book to honor your mother, to heal from her absence, to better understand her sacrifices, or to reflect on your own role as a mother—know this:

Her presence mattered.

Her love was enough.

And what she poured into you still flows through you.

And if this book was given to you as a gift from a son, daughter, or loved one—may every page serve as a reminder that you are *seen*, *valued*, and *deeply appreciated*. Let this be something you can open again and again, cherishing the honor written just for you.

Or perhaps you're the one giving this book—to your mother, your grandmother, or a mother-figure who shaped your life. This gift is more than a keepsake—it's a permanent "thank you," a living tribute wrapped in words that echo the gratitude you feel.

Let's honor her—not just in memory, not just in moments, but in the way we live.

Let's honor the power of her presence.

— *Ethan L. Ketterer*

Table of Contents

Chapter 1

The Power That Didn't Speak Loud

Not all power roars.

Some power whispers.

Some power simply walks into a room and everything shifts—not because of noise, but because of *presence*.

My mother had that kind of power.

Her power wasn't about volume. It wasn't wrapped in flashy words or grand gestures. It didn't come from a stage or spotlight. Her power lived in the details—in the things the world often overlooks. It showed up in the way she moved through each day, handling life's weight with grace, dignity, and unshakable determination.

She wasn't a superhero, but she had superpowers.

She didn't wear a cape, but she carried a household.

She didn't ask for praise, but she lived in a way that deserved it every single day.

I didn't realize at the time that I was watching greatness. As a child, I thought I was simply growing up in a regular home. But now I know—I was being raised in the presence of quiet excellence. She was a master of endurance. A professor of resilience. A champion of love.

She had a way of creating peace even when chaos was close. She didn't need to yell to be heard—her presence alone commanded respect. Her consistency taught us what stability looked like. And her love—though it wasn't always spoken in poetic terms—was undeniable. It wrapped itself around us like a warm blanket in a cold world.

She taught me that you don't have to be loud to be powerful.

You don't have to be seen to be significant.

You don't have to be celebrated to be impactful.

Her kind of power doesn't trend on social media. It doesn't win awards. It doesn't go viral.

But it *changes lives*.

Every meal cooked with tired hands…

Every ride given when gas was low and patience lower…

Every tear wiped when she herself had reasons to cry…

Every sacrifice made without complaint…

All of it was power in motion. A love language without words. A faith that showed up, even when her strength was running low.

She gave, and then gave some more. Not because she had extra, but because she believed her family deserved her best—even if it cost her everything. She covered us with prayers, protected us with her presence, and pushed us forward with her unwavering belief that we were meant for more.

And here's what I've come to understand—**there is a sacred strength in women who lead with love**. A holy power in mothers who give their all and ask for nothing in return. A divine resilience in the ones who raise children while holding their own brokenness behind their backs.

When I think of my mother, I don't remember long speeches or dramatic moments. I remember the way she looked at me when I was struggling. The way she hugged me when words failed. The way she showed up again and again when she had every excuse not to.

Even in the stillness, she was speaking.

Even in the silence, she was teaching.

Even in her absence now, she's still guiding.

Her legacy didn't require a microphone. It required moments—small, sacred moments that added up to a lifetime of love and leadership.

To every mother who feels unseen…

To every woman who has given more than she's received…

To every heart that has kept beating for others when no one was beating for her…

This chapter is for you.

You are the power that didn't speak loud—but your presence still speaks.

You may not hear the applause, but heaven hears your prayers.

You may not feel celebrated, but you are not forgotten.

The world may never know your name.

But your children?Your family?

Your legacy?

They will never forget your power.

Chapter Reflection: The Power That Didn't Speak Loud

Scripture Reflection – KJV

"Strength and honour are her clothing; and she shall rejoice in time to come."
— Proverbs 31:25

Reflection Prompt

Think of a time your mother (or a mother-figure) showed strength without words.

What did you learn from her quiet power?

How has her presence continued to guide you, even in her silence?

Write your reflection below:

My Reflection

Chapter 2

A Presence That Built Me

There are some women who shape nations and movements—and others who shape homes and hearts. My mother was the latter. And yet, in shaping our home, I believe she

impacted the world—because she shaped *me*.

She wasn't a builder by trade, but by calling.

She didn't work with concrete or beams, but with belief, sacrifice, and steady presence.

She didn't raise her voice often, but her life spoke volumes.

My mother built me in ways I didn't understand until long after the foundation had already been laid. I didn't see it then—but now I realize: I am standing on a life she constructed with bare hands and bowed knees.

She built me without asking for credit.

She built me without needing thanks.

She built me when no one else even knew I needed to be built.

She was laying bricks in the silence—covering cracks with compassion, framing character with discipline, and anchoring everything in love. Not the kind of love that always felt soft and easy—but the kind that held firm through struggle, sacrifice, and storms.

She never labeled herself as a teacher—but I learned more from watching her than I ever did in a classroom.
She never called herself a counselor—but her quiet encouragement guided me through countless crossroads.
She never claimed to be a preacher—but her life was a gospel of grace, grit, and goodness.

There were days when I thought she was just "being a mom." Now I know—she was constructing legacy.

When she walked through the house fixing broken things, she was teaching me how to mend.
When she sat in silence after a long day, she was showing me how to carry pain without passing it on.
When she showed up—over and over—without fanfare, she was building something eternal in me.

She gave structure to my soul.

She added strength to my spine.

She helped me believe that love doesn't have to shout to be real. It just has to *remain*.

I remember one particular winter—money was tight, and there wasn't much under the tree. But somehow, there was warmth in the room. Peace in our hearts. Joy in our voices. She made sure of it. She filled the house with something no gift could give. And years later, I realized— what she gave us wasn't material. It was *miraculous*.

That's the kind of builder she was.

And now, whenever someone compliments my kindness, my wisdom, or my work ethic—I know it's not just me they're seeing. They're seeing *her hands* at work in me. They're hearing *her voice* through mine. They're feeling the influence of a woman who never needed to be center stage to make an impact.

She showed me how to build others.

How to speak life.

How to hold space for someone's growth—just like she did for mine.

And if your mother, or any mother-figure in your life, ever made sure you had what you needed even when she didn't… if she stayed when others left, if she gave when it cost her, if she spoke gently when the world was harsh—then she built something sacred in you, too.

Because the truth is, some of the strongest foundations were laid by women whose names will never be in textbooks, but whose love changed lives.

They built character.

They built vision.

They built warriors—with their presence alone.

And if you're reading this and missing her, or wishing you could thank her one more time, let this be your offering: **live well in what she built.**

Let her sacrifices not be in vain.

Let her strength be your strength.

Let her presence be the echo that steadies you when life shakes your core.

Because she didn't just love you.

She built you.

And that kind of presence—whether remembered, embraced, or deeply missed—is the kind that never stops holding you up.

Chapter Reflection: A Presence That Built Me

Scripture Reflection – KJV

"Every wise woman buildeth her house: but the foolish plucketh it down with her hands."

— Proverbs 14:1

Reflection Prompt

Who built you—not through words, but through presence?

What moments of quiet sacrifice or steady love have stayed with you the longest?

Write about how her unseen efforts became your foundation.

Write your reflection below:

My Reflection

Chapter 3

When Her Eyes Spoke Volumes

Some people speak with power. Others speak with wisdom.

But a rare few speak with nothing at all—and are still heard loud and clear.

My mother's eyes could tell a whole story.

She didn't need paragraphs. She didn't need to raise her voice.

One glance could change your attitude. One look could call you back to yourself.

Her eyes were never cruel, but they were **corrective**, **compassionate**, and **cutting all at once**.

Before I ever truly understood what sacrifice looked like, I saw it in her eyes.

When we had less, but she gave more…

When she was hurting, but smiled anyway…

When she was exhausted, but still pressed on…

Her eyes gave her away.

They told the truth even when her mouth didn't.

I can still remember being a child and catching a glimpse of her in the mirror when she thought no one was watching. Her eyes looked tired. Not just from the day, but from the weight she carried. But the moment we locked eyes—just for a second—she smiled.
She never wanted her weariness to dim our light.

She bore burdens in her bones, but never passed them on.

And yet, when I needed it, her look could check me faster than any punishment.

That *"don't you dare"* look at church.

The *"you know better"* glance at the store.

The *"you're embarrassing yourself"* stare when I got out of line.

I learned to straighten up based on her eyebrows alone.

She had mastered the language of restraint.

She didn't need to lecture. Her eyes had lived long enough to speak for her.

They held decades of wisdom, faith, disappointment, and hope—and they taught me how to listen to what *wasn't said.*

As I got older, her eyes became even more meaningful.

I began to notice when they filled with tears—sometimes for reasons she'd never speak aloud.
I noticed when they lit up with pride, even if she said nothing.

And I noticed when they searched my face, trying to make sure I was okay without needing to ask.

Her eyes were her voice, her presence, her power.

Even now, I sometimes close my eyes and see hers.

I see them when I'm faced with a decision.

I see them when I'm tempted to settle.

I see them when I need strength to keep going.

They remind me of who I am.

Of who I belong to.

Of who poured too much into me for me to give up now.

It's amazing how a mother's glance can linger long after she's gone.

How one look can become a lesson.

How one moment of eye contact can correct, cover, and connect all at once.

And maybe you've had a mother like that too.

Maybe she wasn't expressive with her words, but you always knew what she meant.

Maybe she didn't write you long letters, but her look said, "I love you," "I'm proud of you," and "Be careful out there."

Maybe you still feel those eyes on you—when you need them most.

If so, you know what I mean when I say:

Her eyes didn't just watch you. They watched *over* you.

They guarded your growth.

They warned you when danger was close.

They stayed on you—even when you tried to act like you didn't care.

But deep down? You did.

Because her eyes were home. Her eyes were truth.

Her eyes spoke volumes—and they still do.

Chapter Reflection: When Her Eyes Spoke Volumes

Scripture Reflection – KJV

"The light of the eyes rejoiceth the heart: and a good report maketh the bones fat."

— Proverbs 15:30

Reflection Prompt

What's a moment you remember your mother (or mother-figure) using just her eyes to guide you?
How did that look shape your behavior or decisions?
What did her eyes say that words never could?

Write your reflection below:

My Reflection

Chapter 4

Her Sacrifices, My Survival

There are some things we don't truly understand until we're older.
Not because they were hidden— But because we weren't yet mature enough to see them clearly.

My mother's sacrifices were like that.

At the time, they looked like routine. Like just "what moms do." But they weren't routine—they were revolutionary. She was giving up pieces of herself to keep our world spinning. She was placing bricks on the path beneath our feet while walking barefoot herself.

She did it without complaining. Without explaining.

She just did it. Because *we mattered more to her than anything she had to give up.*

And now, as I reflect back, I see it all so vividly.

I remember the winter when the heat barely worked, and she gave us the best blankets while she layered up in silence.

I remember the meals where she "wasn't hungry"—but it wasn't because she'd already eaten. It was because she made sure we had enough.

I remember the clothes she wore year after year so we could go back to school with something new.

She sacrificed in ways that never made the news, but that built the news of *my* life.

She didn't get a day off. There was no retirement plan. No awards. No applause.

But every one of her sacrifices echoed through the choices I got to make.

Through the doors I got to walk through.

Through the opportunities I never had to question.

Her "no" made room for my "yes."

Her delay created space for my destiny.

Her silence made way for my survival.

And let's be honest—some of her sacrifices weren't just practical. They were personal. Emotional. Deep.

She had to swallow grief so we wouldn't feel it.

She held back anger so we wouldn't inherit it.

She stifled dreams so we could chase our own.

And still, she never made us feel like a burden.

She never let her fatigue become our guilt.

She gave joy even while carrying sorrow.

That is the definition of strength.

That is the quiet miracle of motherhood.

I now understand why she moved the way she did—why she made choices that didn't make sense to me at the time.

She was building a future with her sacrifice as the soil.

She was investing in a legacy that would outlive her.

And I was that legacy.

I survived because she endured.

I thrived because she went without.

I stood tall because she knelt in prayer.

And now, as I live the life she helped make possible, I do so with deep reverence.

Because I know I'm walking in the shadow of her sacrifices.

Every win, every step, every breakthrough—I trace it back to her.

So to the mothers who went without so their children could have…

To the women who didn't get to chase every dream because they were too busy protecting someone else's…

To the givers, the stretchers, the quiet warriors who never ask for recognition…

You are seen.

You are honored.

And your sacrifices are not forgotten.

Because we're still standing because of what you gave up.

We're still rising because of the tears you never let fall in front of us.

We are here—**because you stayed.**

And even if the world doesn't always say it, we will:

Thank you. We survived because of you.

Chapter Reflection: Her Sacrifices, My Survival

Scripture Reflection – KJV

"She looketh well to the ways of her household, and eateth not the bread of idleness."
— Proverbs 31:27

Reflection Prompt

What is one sacrifice your mother (or mother-figure) made that you couldn't appreciate until later in life?
How did that act of love contribute to your growth, peace, or survival?

Write your reflection below:

My Reflection

Chapter 5

Lessons from the Kitchen Table

There are some classrooms where the teacher never raises her voice, the lessons aren't written on a board, and there's no test at the end—but somehow, you learn everything you need to know.

My mother's kitchen table was that kind of classroom.

It wasn't fancy.

Sometimes it wobbled. Sometimes it was cluttered.

But it was holy.

That table carried the weight of every joy and every struggle.

It heard laughter. It held tears. It bore witness to dreams being spoken out loud for the first time—and to disappointments no one else knew about.

It was a table, yes—but also a sanctuary.

That's where she taught us the values that no textbook could cover:

How to give thanks, even when the portions were small.

How to speak gently, even when emotions were high.

How to clean up not just after meals—but after ourselves, our mistakes, and our attitudes.

She didn't lecture us like a professor. She just lived wisdom in front of us—every single day.

Some mornings, we rushed by that table, grabbing food before heading out the door. But on the days when life slowed down just enough for us to sit with her? That's when the best lessons came. That's when she'd talk about what was going on in the world, and in our hearts. And somehow, without judgment, she'd guide us back to center.

She used questions like tools:

"How was your day?"

"What happened at school?"

"What did you learn today?"

And sometimes—"What are you not telling me?"

She didn't need a degree in psychology. She just *knew*. She could read between our words. She could hear what we *weren't* saying. And no matter what it was, she always made room at the table for it. For *us*.

I remember the times when I didn't want to talk—when I thought I could hide my pain behind silence. But she'd place a warm plate in front of me, sit down, and just… wait. And in that silence, I felt safe. Eventually, the words would come. Sometimes with tears. Sometimes with relief. But they always came—because she made it safe to speak.

She taught me that healing doesn't always require answers. Sometimes, it just needs *presence*.

And then there were the lessons about grace.

The times I messed up—and knew I had.

The times when I deserved discipline—but instead, she gave me understanding.

The moments when she could have turned her back—but instead, she made me a plate and said, "Eat first, we'll talk after."

It was at that table that I learned forgiveness.

It was at that table that I learned dignity.

It was at that table that I learned what *home* really meant.

She didn't quote scripture at every meal, but she lived it in front of us.

She didn't recite proverbs, but she embodied them.

She didn't need to remind us that love was present—we could taste it in the food, hear it in her tone, and feel it in her eyes.

And even when the food was simple—rice and beans, bread and butter, leftovers that didn't look like much— her love seasoned it so richly that we never left the table feeling empty.

That's why I say she preached from the kitchen table. Not with a pulpit, but with purpose.

And today, as I sit at my own table, or as I hear others share their stories, I often return to that small, sacred space where so much of who I am was formed.

The table wasn't where life paused.

It was where it made sense.

And if you had a mother or grandmother or guardian who cooked for you, waited up for you, or sat quietly with you after a hard day—then you know what I mean.

You know the power of that table.

You know the peace that lived there.

You know the lessons that were served alongside every plate.

Because she wasn't just feeding you.

She was forming you.

And those meals? Those moments?

They're still feeding you now.

I still remember the moments when we finished dinner, and the conversation would drift to dreams and aspirations. She would lean forward, her eyes gleaming with encouragement, asking me what I wanted to become.

It was as if the weight of the world dissolved in those precious exchanges.

The kitchen table was not just for meals; it became a launchpad for ambitions, where ideas took flight under her watchful gaze.

There were days she'd share stories from her own childhood—fables of resilience and determination that shaped her own journey. She spoke of the small town she grew up in, the challenges she faced orphaned young, and how every hurdle was a lesson in disguise.

I hung onto every word, feeling her past intertwine with my future. She spoke of hardships but always sprinkled hope throughout.

"You can do anything, but it requires hard work, patience, and a heart full of kindness," she'd say, her voice steady yet gentle.

As I navigated life's challenges, her lessons rang in my ears like a favorite melody—an anthem of strength and perseverance. The kitchen table transformed into a realm where I learned that failures were merely stepping stones, not dead ends. We would sit in that timeless space, discussing the importance of integrity and character, realizing that true success wasn't measured merely by accolades, but by the lives touched along the way.

Each meal wasn't just about nourishment;

It was about sharing goals, fears, and hopes, stitched seamlessly into the fabric of our lives.

Chapter Reflection: Lessons from the Kitchen Table

Scripture Reflection – KJV

"Better is a dinner of herbs where love is, than a stalled ox and hatred therewith."

— Proverbs 15:17

Reflection Prompt

What are some of the most powerful moments you experienced around a kitchen or dining table?
How did your mother or a mother-figure use food, conversation, or presence to teach, guide, or nurture you?

Write your reflection below:

My Reflection

Chapter 6

Grace Under Pressure

You don't truly understand grace until you watch someone live through something that should have broken them—and they still show up with love in their hands and peace in their eyes.

That was my mother.

She was never loud about what she carried.

She didn't broadcast her burdens.

She didn't collapse in front of us—even when life gave

her every reason to.

She just kept moving. Kept managing. Kept mothering.

But what looked like effortless strength was really **grace under pressure**.

I watched her hold life together when it was falling apart behind the scenes.

I saw her manage a household with pennies while still making it feel like abundance.

I witnessed her make hard decisions—decisions that no one applauded—just to protect us from the harshness she herself had to endure.

There was a time when the refrigerator was nearly empty, but she made a meal stretch like it was a feast.
There was a time the electricity was cut off, and she lit candles like we were having a special evening instead of shielding us from embarrassment.

There were days when we didn't know how close we were to the edge—but she stood tall, smiled soft, and made it seem like everything was okay.

And in those moments, I learned something sacred:
Strength doesn't always show up in loud, visible ways. Sometimes, it looks like gentleness that refuses to break.

That's grace.

Grace is what allowed her to take deep breaths instead of shouting when stress was heavy.

Grace is what helped her forgive offenses without revenge.

Grace is what held her steady when life was spinning, children were crying, bills were mounting, and her body was tired.

She didn't always quote scripture, but she lived it.
"Be still and know that I am God." She embodied it.
"Let not your heart be troubled." She practiced it.

And what I understand now is that grace under pressure isn't weakness.

It's *supernatural strength* clothed in humility.

It's choosing peace when chaos is easier.

It's standing firm when surrender would be justified.

It's smiling not because you feel like it, but because someone in your house needs hope—and you decide to become that hope.

That's what my mother did.

She became the peace in the pressure.

She became the calm in the storm.

She became the steady when everything else was shifting.

And even in the silence, she was teaching us.

Teaching us how to suffer with dignity.

Teaching us how to pray instead of panic.

Teaching us how to *lead with love, even when life is unfair.*

Now when I'm facing my own storms—when money's tight, when relationships strain, when work becomes heavy—I remember her.

I remember how she responded to pressure.
And I realize: I am who I am because I saw how she endured.

She didn't tell us she was tired—she just kept going.
She didn't complain about unfairness—she just kept building.
She didn't demand recognition—she just kept showing up.

That's grace.

Grace that doesn't need an audience.

Grace that holds you together when everything else is pulling you apart.

And maybe you've seen that too.

Maybe your mother, grandmother, aunt, or guardian carried burdens you didn't even recognize until you got older.
Maybe she carried trauma, heartbreak, injustice, or deep fatigue—and still made a way.

Maybe she gave you strength not just by what she said, but by *how she survived.*

If that's your story, then you know that some of life's greatest lessons don't come from what a mother teaches you—they come from how she *lives in front of you.*

She didn't just talk about grace.

She became it.

And that's why we honor her. Not just because of what she did—but because of how she did it.

With grace.

With love.

Under pressure.

Chapter Reflection: Grace Under Pressure

Scripture Reflection – KJV

"And he said unto me, My grace is sufficient for thee: for my strength is made perfect in weakness."

— 2 Corinthians 12:9

Reflection Prompt

Think of a time when a mother or mother-figure in your life carried herself with quiet strength through difficult circumstances. What did that moment teach you about grace, resilience, or faith? How has her example helped you endure life's pressures?

Write your reflection below:

My Reflection

Chapter 7

She Prayed Me Through

There's a kind of protection that doesn't come from alarms, locks, or shields.

It comes from *prayer*.

And the strongest covering I've ever known was my mother's whispered prayers.

She didn't pray for attention.

She didn't pray to impress.

She prayed because it was *how she fought*.

For many years, I didn't understand it. I thought she was just being quiet.

But now I know—while I was sleeping, she was *interceding*.

While I was out chasing things that didn't matter, she was on her knees asking God to keep me from ruining my future.

While I was ignoring her advice, she was still calling my name in the presence of God.

She didn't raise her voice in front of crowds, but she raised a cry in the presence of the Lord.

And her prayers did what lectures, rules, and even consequences couldn't do—they reached my soul.

There were seasons of my life when I should've gone down paths I had no business walking.

But doors I was trying to push open stayed shut. Distractions I chased fell apart before they could trap me. Trouble got close—but didn't touch me.

And now I understand: **it wasn't coincidence. It was covering.**

Her prayers were invisible, but they were powerful.

They built a wall I didn't know I needed.

They opened doors I wasn't strong enough to knock on. They softened my heart when the world tried to harden it.

I remember hearing her pray behind closed doors—no fanfare, no noise.

Just her voice in the early hours of the morning or late at night:

"God, help my children."

"God, protect them from what they can't see."

"God, don't let them lose their way."

"God, please… just cover them."

She didn't just pray when things went wrong.

She prayed *before* we knew they could.

That's how much she believed in the power of prayer.

That's how much she believed in the God who listens.

And what I didn't realize then, I treasure now:

My growth, my recovery, my ability to stand when life tries to knock me down—it all traces back to her faith.
To her bending knees.

To her whispered words.

To her belief that even when she couldn't reach us, *God still could*.

She wasn't perfect. But she was powerful in prayer. She didn't always know what to say to us in conversation—but she always knew what to say to God. And that's what saved me.

Her prayers followed me into every room I walked into.

They softened hearts on my behalf.

They changed outcomes.

They reminded me of who I was when I forgot.

Because a praying mother doesn't just raise a child—**she launches a destiny.**

Maybe you had a mother, grandmother, aunt, or guardian who did the same.

Maybe you've never heard her say it—but you felt it. You felt covered. You felt protected. You felt *called* back to something deeper.

That's what happens when a mother prays.

And maybe she's not here anymore. Maybe her voice has faded in your ears.

But the echoes of her intercession still linger.
Because prayer never dies—it outlives the one who spoke it.

So if you've made it this far, don't just thank God for your strength.

Thank Him for the one who prayed you through.

Because long before you stood in your strength,
she stood in the gap.

Chapter Reflection: She Prayed Me Through

Scripture Reflection – KJV

"The effectual fervent prayer of a righteous man availeth much."

— James 5:16b

Reflection Prompt

Think about the role prayer has played in your life. Who prayed for you when you didn't have the strength or wisdom to pray for yourself? How have those prayers shaped your direction, your protection, and your purpose?

Write your reflection below:

My Reflection

Chapter 8

The Foundation Beneath My Feet

I didn't always realize it.

But now I do:

I've never walked alone.

Even when I thought I was standing on my own two feet—

Even when I thought I was grown, capable, independent—

I was standing on something **she built.**

My mother wasn't just present.

She was foundational.

She was the unseen strength beneath every success.
The quiet support behind every breakthrough.
The reason I could stand tall, even when life tried to bring me low.

She was the reason I didn't crumble.

You see, some mothers hold your hand while you walk. Others?

They become the ground you walk on.

That was her.

She became my starting place, my safety net, my moral compass, my spiritual springboard.

She didn't just love me.

She **anchored** me.

Every "be respectful" when I didn't want to listen…

Every "you better fix your tone" when pride tried to rise…
Every time she made me go back and do it right instead of letting me slide by—

That wasn't control.

That was construction.

She was laying bricks beneath me.

Bricks of **discipline.**

Bricks of **humility.**

Bricks of **accountability.**

Bricks of **God-first values.**

At the time, it felt like pressure.

But now? I realize it was purpose.

She knew that one day, I'd have to make decisions without her voice in the next room.

And so she built a voice inside of me that would never leave.

A voice that said:

"You don't cut corners."

"You don't lie to get ahead."

"You show up, even when it's hard."

"You treat people right—even when they don't return it."

"You walk with integrity—even when no one's watching."

That's what she gave me—not just love, but **limits.**

Not just encouragement, but **expectations.**

Not just faith, but a **framework** to live by.

And now that she's no longer here physically, I understand something deeper:

Her presence was never meant to stay next to me—it was meant to live beneath me.

She didn't just teach me how to survive—she built me to *stand.*

Stand in truth.

Stand in faith.

Stand in responsibility.

Stand for something greater than myself.

And what amazes me the most is that she never asked for credit.

She didn't need me to recognize what she was doing. She just did it—quietly, faithfully, completely.

And I wonder how many mothers do the same.

How many women pour into their children day after day…

How many hold back tears so they can stay strong for someone else…

How many set boundaries, not because they're harsh, but because they're building something beneath the surface?

Because a true foundation doesn't always get attention. It doesn't shine.

It doesn't speak.

But when storms come, **it's what holds everything together.**

And that's what she was for me.

The reason I didn't break when life tried to shake me.

The reason I could rebuild when life knocked me down.

The reason I kept going—even when I didn't think I had anything left.

If you had a mother like that—someone who poured into you more than she poured into herself—then you're walking on something sacred.

You are standing on strength that didn't start with you. You are living a life that was first prayed for, paid for, *and built* by someone else.

And today, I honor her.

Not just for who she was—but for what she built beneath me.

Because even when I couldn't see it,
her love was holding me up.

Chapter Reflection: The Foundation Beneath My Feet

Scripture Reflection – KJV

"Train up a child in the way he should go: and when he is old, he will not depart from it."

— Proverbs 22:6

Reflection Prompt

Who in your life laid the moral, emotional, or spiritual foundation that still supports you today? What values did they instill that continue to guide your decisions and keep you grounded?

Write your reflection below:

My Reflection

Chapter 9

The Day I Realized She Was Right

There's a shift that happens—not always loudly, and rarely all at once.

But one day, life plays back your mother's voice in your head…
And suddenly, everything clicks.

She was right.

She wasn't just nagging.

She wasn't trying to ruin my fun.

She wasn't being overprotective or "old-fashioned."

She was **seeing ahead of me**.

And now that I've walked a few miles down life's road, I can admit—there were countless moments where I thought I knew better.

I dismissed her warnings.

I rolled my eyes at her concerns.

I thought, "She just doesn't get it."

But she got it.

She got **all of it.**

What looked like restrictions were really *rescue attempts*.

What felt like lectures were *life preservers*.

What sounded like fear was actually **foresight**.

And the day I realized she was right wasn't some huge revelation—it was a slow awareness, built brick by brick through experience.

- The day I trusted someone she told me to watch and got burned…
- The day I took a risk she cautioned against and paid for it with consequences…
- The day I found myself whispering her words to someone else, realizing I now believed the very things I once rejected…

It humbled me.

Because what I once treated as nagging advice—I now see as **prophetic love**.

She saw dangers I couldn't.

She knew how fast time moves, how painful wrong turns are, how lonely the world can be when you don't listen to wisdom.

She had lived through storms I hadn't even felt the raindrops of yet.

And she wasn't trying to control me—

She was trying to **keep me from having to learn everything the hard way**.

That's what love does. It speaks—even when it's ignored.

It shows up—even when it's rejected.

It doesn't throw your mistakes back at you—it reaches out and pulls you in.

I'll never forget the first time I truly failed after going against her advice.

I expected distance. I expected disappointment.

Instead, I got a seat at the table. A hug. A soft "I knew, but I had to let you grow."

That was love. That was grace. That was **the lesson and the covering—together**.

And it changed how I saw her forever.

She hadn't been trying to be right for her own sake.
She was trying to make sure I'd still be standing when life proved her right.

That's the kind of wisdom you only appreciate with time.

And now I find myself quoting her—often.

Not just to others, but to myself.

Her words show up when I'm tired, when I'm tempted, when I'm tested.

They become a mirror, a map, and a reminder of the depth of her love.

Because the truth is: she was never just trying to be right about rules—

She was right about *me*.

Right about the potential she saw in me.

Right about the calling over my life.

Right about what I was capable of, and what could derail it.

And for every warning, every raised eyebrow, every piece of advice I once brushed off—

I now say: *Thank you.*

You were right.

And I didn't always say it, but I see it now.

And I *carry it now*.

Chapter Reflection: The Day I Realized She Was Right

Scripture Reflection – KJV

"Hearken unto thy father that begat thee, and despise not thy mother when she is old."

— Proverbs 23:22

Reflection Prompt

What wisdom from your mother (or a mother-figure) did you resist or reject when you were younger, only to realize later she was right? How has that moment shaped the way you make decisions today?

Write your reflection below:

My Reflection

Chapter 10

She Showed Me What Love Looks Like

Love isn't always loud.

It doesn't always come dressed in flowers and gifts.

Sometimes, love wears house shoes.

Sometimes, it stands over a stove.

Sometimes, it waits quietly in a hallway, praying for your safe return.

She showed me what love looks like.

Not with dramatic speeches.

Not with picture-perfect moments.

But in the day-to-day, minute-by-minute choices she made.

She loved us with her time, when she had none to spare.

She loved us with her presence, even when her heart was heavy.

She loved us with her strength, when life kept trying to wear her down.

She didn't have to say, "I love you" every day—because she lived it every day.

Love looked like making sure we ate, even when she wasn't hungry.

Love looked like pressing our clothes before work or school while she wore the same pair of shoes until they wore thin.

Love looked like waking up early and going to bed last, just to keep everything and everyone together.

Her love didn't ask for attention.

It just **showed up**—again and again and again.

She loved us in ways that didn't always look like love to a child—

- Like discipline when we wanted permission.
- Like silence when we wanted answers.
- Like boundaries when we wanted freedom.

But now?

Now I understand.

Now I see that love was never just about feelings—it was about foundation.

She gave stability in a world that didn't always feel secure.

She gave peace, even when she was battling storms of her own.

Her love was **faith in action**.

It was commitment without conditions.

It was generosity that didn't come from abundance—but from *sacrifice*.

And the most remarkable thing?

She never made us feel like a burden.

Never made us feel guilty for the weight she carried.

Never once made us question whether or not we were worth it.

Because to her, we were always worth it.

When the world overlooked us, she lifted us.
When we failed, she forgave faster than we could ask.
When we got too grown to listen, she still watched over us from a distance—with love that never wavered.

She didn't love with limits.

She loved with legacy.

And now, when I love others—with patience, with presence, with consistency—I realize:

I'm loving the way she taught me.

The way she lived it.

The way she breathed it.

Her love wasn't performative—it was powerful.

It wasn't flawless—it was faithful.

It wasn't always seen—but it was *always there.*

And if your mother or mother-figure ever loved you like that—quietly, deeply, sacrificially—then you know.

You know the way it changes you.

You know the way it becomes a part of how you see the world.

You know that kind of love never dies—it *dwells*.

So no, she didn't just love me.

She showed me what love *is*.

Chapter Reflection: She Showed Me What Love Looks Like

Scripture Reflection – KJV

"My little children, let us not love in word, neither in tongue; but in deed and in truth."

— 1 John 3:18

Reflection Prompt

Think about the quiet, consistent ways your mother or another woman in your life demonstrated love. How did those actions speak louder than words? How are you now showing that kind of love to others?

Write your reflection below:

My Reflection

Chapter 11

She Didn't Need a Stage

The world tells us to chase visibility.

To build a following.

To climb a ladder.

To be seen, heard, and celebrated.

But she?

She didn't need a stage.

Her life wasn't about applause—it was about *assignment*.

She wasn't performing.

She was pouring.

Pouring her love into her family.

Pouring her time into her children.

Pouring her wisdom into conversations that may have felt small in the moment—but ended up shaping lifetimes.

She didn't need to stand behind a podium.

She stood behind the scenes—quiet, steady, committed.

She didn't need a mic to be heard.

Her actions were loud enough.

The meals she made.

The nights she stayed up.

The prayers she whispered.

The sacrifices she made with no parade, no "thank you," no crowd watching—**that was her platform.**

And it was enough.

She never asked for recognition.

She didn't measure her value by who noticed.

She just showed up, every single day.

Not because it was easy.

Not because she had to.

But because she *chose* to.

Because she believed in legacy more than limelight.

She was content being the backbone, the anchor, the heart of our home—even if nobody ever gave her a standing ovation for it.

And the irony?

Now that I'm older…

Now that I've walked through storms…

Now that I've tried to hold things together with my own hands…

I realize she was the strongest, most influential person

I've ever known.

She didn't chase the spotlight, but she lit the room.
She didn't crave influence, but she changed lives.
She didn't demand respect, but she earned it—quietly, consistently, humbly.

She was never the loudest in the room, but her absence would have left the biggest silence.

And that's the kind of strength we don't celebrate enough.

The kind that doesn't trend.

The kind that doesn't wear titles.

The kind that happens in kitchens, in hospital waiting rooms, in late-night phone calls, in whispered prayers, and over tired shoulders.

She built her life on faithfulness, not fame.

She didn't need to be invited to the stage—**she made every room holy with her presence.**

So now, when I see people chasing accolades, recognition, and applause—I think of her.

And I remember: true impact doesn't need an audience.

True impact is felt, not flaunted.

It's lived, not posted.

It's passed down, not performed.

If you had a mother like that—a woman who never tried to be seen, but somehow became unforgettable—then you know the power of humility.

You know the beauty of quiet love.

You know the strength of someone who showed up, even when no one saw her doing it.

She didn't need to be "known."

She just needed her love to be felt.

And it was.

And it still is.

Because the greatest stages aren't always made of wood and lights.

Sometimes, the greatest stages are made of memories. Of legacy.

Of love.

And that's the stage she stood on every day—whether we saw it or not.

Chapter Reflection: She Didn't Need a Stage

Scripture Reflection – KJV

"Let nothing be done through strife or vainglory; but in lowliness of mind let each esteem other better than themselves."
— Philippians 2:3

Reflection Prompt

Who are the quiet heroes in your life—those who made a difference without needing recognition? How can you honor their example by serving with humility, consistency, and love that doesn't need the spotlight?

Write your reflection below:

My Reflection

Chapter 12

More Than a Provider

When we're young, we tend to measure provision by what we can see.

The meals on the table.

The clothes on our backs.

The lights that stay on and the shoes that fit just right.

And for a long time, I thought that's what made her a provider—how she met our needs.

But the older I got, the more I understood:

She was more than a provider.

She didn't just put things in our hands.

She put strength in our hearts.

She didn't just keep the house running.

She kept our *faith* running.

She didn't just provide shelter.

She provided *security. Stability. Sanity.*

Because she knew:

It wasn't enough to just give us food—she had to feed our soul.

It wasn't enough to clothe our bodies—she had to cover our future.

It wasn't enough to help us grow up—she wanted us to grow strong.

She did that without a roadmap, without applause, and often without a break.

She was the reason I had a safe place to fall.

The reason I could walk into the world with confidence.

The reason I believed I could be something more— because she saw it in me first.

And sometimes, she gave us *everything* while holding onto nothing for herself.

I remember times she made our plates first, only to "not be hungry" later.

Or the nights she stayed up with us, sacrificing her rest just to make sure we had peace.

Or how she always seemed to make a way—even when resources were tight—because giving up wasn't part of her vocabulary.

But what struck me most as I got older wasn't what she *bought*—

It was what she *built*.

She built structure in our lives.

She built expectations, not to burden us—but to build character.

She built hope when things felt uncertain.
She built resilience—one steady act of love at a time.

And even when she was tired, she gave us her energy.

Even when she was worried, she gave us her calm.

Even when she was overlooked, she made sure we felt seen.

She poured into us with words, hugs, chores, prayers, sacrifices, and hard lessons.

She never ran out of love, even when she ran out of sleep.

She never withheld warmth, even when life was cold to her.

Because to her, provision wasn't just about paychecks.

It was about being present.

It was about preparing us for a world that wouldn't always be gentle.

It was about protecting us in every way she knew how— even when we didn't recognize it.

And that's why I say she was *more than a provider*.

She was a lifeline.

A counselor.

A storm-shielder.

A legacy builder.

Her love didn't just meet our needs—it made us whole.

And now, when I find myself showing up for someone, choosing selflessness, or giving grace instead of anger—I realize…

I'm walking in what she gave.

I'm standing on what she built.

I'm living out the provision that started with her.

So if you had a mother, grandmother, aunt, or guardian who gave you more than you could ever repay—who gave without limits, taught without pride, and loved without conditions—then you know what I mean when I say:

She was more than a provider.

She was a presence that still provides.

Chapter Reflection: More Than a Provider

Scripture Reflection – KJV

"Her children arise up, and call her blessed; her husband also, and he praiseth her."

— Proverbs 31:28

Reflection Prompt

What are some non-material ways your mother or a mother-figure provided for you? Think about how her presence, her encouragement, and her emotional or spiritual sacrifices became the foundation of your life. How are you paying that forward today?

Write your reflection below:

My Reflection

Chapter 13: A Presence That Still Covers Me

There are some voices that fade over time—and others that echo louder with every passing year.

Her voice is one of them.

Even though I can no longer hear it in the room,
I still hear it in the **rhythms of my life.**

In the choices I make.

In the lessons I apply.

In the still, small moments when I whisper her words to
myself for strength.

Because even though she's not physically beside me,
her presence still covers me.

She covered me when I was a child with her hands—
Tying my shoes. Braiding my hair. Holding me tight
when the world felt too big.

She covered me in my youth with her prayers—
Some I heard out loud, some I didn't, but all of them
reached heaven.

She covered me in adulthood with her example—
How she walked with dignity. How she endured without
bitterness. How she gave without needing recognition.

And now, even in her absence, I still feel her covering. Not with blankets or warm meals, but with **reminders**:

- *"Be kind—even when others aren't."*
- *"Stand up for yourself—but stay humble."*
- *"Don't let the world change your heart."*

She is in my laughter when I remember her jokes.

She is in my silence when I lean into the strength she taught me.

She is in my wisdom when I give the same advice she once gave me.

Some days, I still reach for the phone.

Still instinctively want to tell her my news.

Still wish I could hear her say, "I'm proud of you."

But then I feel something—deep, quiet, unshakable.

Her presence.

And it covers me like it always has.

Softly.

Steadily.

Sacredly.

She may not be here to speak—but she still speaks.

Through memories.

Through mannerisms.

Through values that guide me like a compass when life feels unsteady.

I hear her in my prayers.

Feel her in my peace.

Sense her when I'm making a decision she would've helped me through.

And that's the beauty of the love she gave—

It didn't expire with time.

It *expanded*.

It rooted itself in who I am, and now it shows up in who I'm becoming.

Because great mothers don't just leave behind belongings—

They leave behind blessings.

And when people ask how I've made it through certain seasons, I smile and say:

"I had a mother who covered me—before, during, and even now."

If your mother is no longer here, and your heart feels the ache of her absence, take comfort in knowing:

What she gave you didn't end when she did.

Her prayers didn't stop.

Her love didn't vanish.

Her lessons didn't lose their power.

You are still walking in the shelter of her sacrifice.
You are still guided by the light of her love.

And every time you rise, speak, pray, lead, give, forgive, or show up for others—

She's still there.

She's still covering you.

And she always will be.

Chapter Reflection: A Presence That Still Covers Me

Scripture Reflection – KJV

"As one whom his mother comforteth, so will I comfort you."

— Isaiah 66:13a

Reflection Prompt

Think about a moment where you felt your mother or a mother-figure's presence after she was gone. What parts of her still guide you today? How can you carry her love forward into the lives of others?

Write your reflection below:

My Reflection

Chapter 14

When I Became Her Reflection

It's a humbling thing to look at your life one day and realize…

You've become her reflection.

Not because you were trying.

Not because you were taught to mimic.

But because her influence was so strong, so steady, so sacred—
That it became part of who you are.

It happened subtly.

In how I close cabinet doors the way she did.
In how I fold clothes while humming one of her favorite songs.
In how I fix someone a plate before fixing my own.
In how I lower my voice when someone's hurting.

I didn't notice it at first.

But the older I got—the more life demanded strength, patience, gentleness, and sacrifice—the more I found myself doing the very things I saw her do.

And not just the surface things.

The soul things.

Like giving grace even when I was the one hurting.
Like holding space for others to fall apart, while holding myself together long enough to help them stand.
Like praying silently while doing dishes or driving—because she taught me that God listens everywhere.

She never sat me down and said, "Do life like this."
She just *lived life like that*.

And I watched.

I absorbed.

And now—I reflect.

I reflect her resilience.

Her wisdom.

Her quiet sense of humor.

Her belief that no matter how hard the day gets, you can still get through it with faith and love.

I used to think, "I'm not her."

We had different personalities. Different styles. Different dreams.

But what I didn't realize then was that being her reflection doesn't mean I lost my identity—
It means her identity left a legacy inside me.

And what an honor that is.

To walk into a room and hear someone say,
"You remind me so much of your mother."
Not because of how I look—

But because of *how I show up.*

When I hold someone's hand in grief.

When I stand up for someone with quiet strength.

When I extend mercy instead of judgment.

When I show up—*not to be seen, but to serve.*

That's her.

That's her reflection in me.

She lives in the way I love people who can't love me back.
She lives in how I forgive others without keeping score.
She lives in how I speak truth gently, the way she used to—correcting but never condemning.

It took years for me to realize that I wasn't just becoming older—I was becoming *her echo.*

Not because I was trying to fill her shoes.
But because her walk through life left footprints too deep not to follow.

So now I carry her everywhere I go.

In my voice.

In my hands.

In my habits.

In my heart.

She taught me that presence isn't about being loud.
It's about being *lasting*.

And now that she's gone, people still feel her—because they feel me.

And through me, they still feel *her*.

If you had a woman like that in your life—a mother, grandmother, aunt, or guardian who shaped you with more than just her words—

Then you know this sacred truth:

When a woman lives well, she lives again through those who carry her legacy.

You become her reflection.

Her extension.

Her living tribute.

And that reflection becomes your strength.

Chapter Reflection: When I Became Her Reflection

Scripture Reflection – KJV

"Her children arise up, and call her blessed..."
— Proverbs 31:28a

Reflection Prompt

What parts of your mother or a mother-figure do you now see in yourself? What attitudes, choices, or values reflect her life and love? How has becoming her reflection changed the way you move through the world?

Write your reflection below:

My Reflection

Chapter 15

The Gift She Left Me

My Brother. My Compass. My Foundation.

When I pause and truly reflect on the greatest gifts my mother gave me,

I find that they're not things I can hold or count or measure.

They don't come with a dollar amount.

They don't collect dust or lose value over time.

They are the kinds of gifts that go **beyond this life**.
Gifts that breathe, guide, and live on in every step I take.

She gave me my brother.

That alone is a blessing that I could never repay.
In him, I see a mirror of the love she poured into both of us.
A reminder that she didn't just give us life—she gave us each other.

She gave us a bond that time, grief, or even silence could never sever.

She gave us a companion for the journey,
someone who understands the parts of our story that no
one else fully could—because he lived them, too.

Whenever I hear his laughter, I hear hers echoing.

Whenever I see his resilience, I see hers rising again.

And in the way he lives, I am constantly reminded:
**She loved us enough to give us life—and she loved us
even more to make that life count.**

But her love didn't stop at giving us to each other.
She didn't just give us family.

She gave us **a moral compass.**

She raised us to understand that doing what's right is not
always easy—but it's always necessary.

That integrity matters when no one is watching.
That truth isn't a matter of convenience, but a way of life.

Her compass wasn't something she handed to us—it was
something we inherited by **watching her.**
How she spoke.

How she handled conflict.

How she remained graceful in hardship.

How she treated people, even when they gave her every reason not to.

She didn't have to tell me to do right—her life was the lesson.
And now, long after her voice has faded from phone calls and rooms, it rises again inside me when I have to make decisions.

Would this make her proud?

Would this reflect what she taught us?

Would this keep her legacy alive?

That's her compass.

Still guiding me.

Still grounding me.

And most of all, she gave us what I now realize was one of the greatest gifts of all:

a proper upbringing.

She didn't raise us in luxury, but she raised us in **order**.

We weren't spoiled with things, but we were enriched with *structure, discipline, and love.*

She gave us expectations—not to limit us, but to lift us.

She taught us how to respect adults.

How to clean up after ourselves.

How to say "please" and "thank you" like we meant it.

How to carry ourselves with decency.

How to represent our home, our name, and God.

There were chores, curfews, corrections, and consequences.

There were standards in our house.
And while we may not have understood them all back then, we now carry the fruit of that foundation in everything we do.

That upbringing didn't just protect us—it **positioned** us.

To walk into rooms with respect.

To make wise decisions.

To take responsibility.

To give without always receiving.

And in every opportunity I now stand in, every relationship I manage, every challenge I navigate—

I hear the echo of her voice, the power of her discipline, and the grace of her example.

My brother.

My moral compass.

My foundation.

Those are the gifts she left me.

They will never fade.

They will never lose relevance.

They will never be forgotten.

And though she may not be here physically,

she is *everywhere* in how I live, how I think, how I love,

and how I lead.

She didn't just leave me with memories—

She left me with meaning.

And that is a gift I will spend my life honoring.

Chapter Reflection: The Gift She Left Me

Scripture Reflection –KJV

"My son, keep thy father's commandment, and forsake not the law of thy mother."

— Proverbs 6:20

Reflection Prompt

What lasting gifts—beyond material things—did your mother or a mother-figure give you? In what ways do they show up in how you carry yourself today? How can you continue her legacy through your actions and choices?

Write your reflection below:

My Reflection

Chapter 16

Because She Loved Us First

(A Love That Built Us)

Before we ever took our first breath,

before we ever knew our names,
before we could offer her anything in return—

She loved us.

She loved us first.

With no conditions.

With no expectations.

With no applause.

Her love didn't wait for us to get things right.
It didn't depend on our grades, our attitudes, or our understanding.

It simply was.

Steady. Constant. Unshakable.

She loved us in a way that made room for our growth.

She loved us in ways we couldn't see until we looked back.

She loved us through our silence, our rebellion, our joy, and our confusion.

And the power of her love was this:

It was always working—even when we didn't recognize it.

It worked in how she protected us from things we didn't even know were threats.

It worked in how she corrected us—not to crush our spirits, but to shape our character.

It worked in how she gave—again and again—even when she was tired, hurting, or empty.

She gave us everything she had without keeping a record of what we owed.

She poured love into us that would one day spill into the lives of others.

And she did it all because she **chose** to love us first.

That love didn't always look like hugs and soft words.

Sometimes it looked like late nights waiting up.

Like phone calls that challenged our decisions.

Like silence that spoke volumes when words weren't needed.

Like boundaries that protected us when we didn't know better.

She loved us with the kind of love that prepared us for life.

Not just for success, but for setbacks.

Not just for moments of celebration, but for seasons of surrender.

Not just for having, but for **giving.**

And now, because she loved us first,

we understand what love really is.

Love isn't just a feeling—it's a commitment.

Love isn't loud—it's loyal.

Love doesn't always show up dressed in grand gestures—

Sometimes, it's quiet, tired, and still present.

Her love taught us that love *stays*.

That it endures.

That it shows up when others walk away.

That it doesn't require perfection—it just keeps showing up.

Because she loved us first…

We learned how to forgive.

We learned how to care.

We learned how to be gentle, and how to be strong.

We learned how to speak life, hold space, and lead with humility.

Her love is still teaching us—

Every time we choose compassion.

Every time we put someone else first.

Every time we sacrifice for those we love.

Every time we stop and say, *"This is what she would've done."*

And now, the love she gave lives on in the way we love others.

In the way we show up for our families.

In the way we protect the people we care about.

In the way we live with meaning, rooted in the truth that…

We were loved into strength.

We were loved into responsibility.

We were loved into becoming who we are today.

So we honor her—

Not just with words or holidays, but by living in a way that reflects her heart.

Because she loved us first—
we now know how to love well.

Chapter Reflection: Because She Loved Us First

Scripture Reflection – KJV

"We love him, because he first loved us."
— *1 John 4:19*

Reflection Prompt

How has your mother or a mother-figure's love shaped the way you show up for others? In what areas of your life do you still feel the echo of her love guiding you forward?

Write your reflection below:

My Reflection

Chapter 17

She Gave Us Her Best

(When Love Looks Like Sacrifice)

She may not have had it all.

She may not have had a village to help her.

She may not have had the luxury of rest or recognition.

But what she had—she gave.

And somehow, she gave it **with everything in her.**
Even when it cost her something, even when it wore her down,
she gave us her best.

She gave us more than food and shelter.

She gave us comfort on sleepless nights.

She gave us correction when we needed it most.

She gave us truth when lies felt easier to believe.

She gave us consistency in a world that didn't always offer stability.

She gave us her **yes**, even when her energy was low.

She gave us her **no**, even when it would've been easier to give in.

She gave us her faith, her focus, her fierce determination to see us become something more than our surroundings.

She gave us her best—

Not because she had everything, but because she had **us.**

And we mattered that much.

We didn't always realize it at the time.

We didn't always notice the way her body ached but she still stood in the kitchen.

We didn't see how the light bill came after the grocery list,

Or how she wore the same shoes for years while we outgrew ours every season.

We just knew things somehow worked out.

And that her love never ran out.

But now we understand…

Her best wasn't in what she bought us.

It was in what she **taught us**:

- That real strength is quiet.
- That love isn't always loud—it's present.
- That showing up, even when it's hard, is a sacred act of love.

She gave us her time when time was short.

She gave us her faith when we had none.

She gave us discipline, not to break us—but to build us.

She gave us protection, even when it meant standing alone.

She gave us resilience by modeling how to rise when life tries to break you.

And she gave it without demanding thanks.

She gave it without asking for applause.

She gave it because **she loved us that much.**

She didn't do it for a reward—

But her reward is in the people we've become.

Because of her, we've learned how to lead with grace.

How to endure with quiet strength.

How to give without expecting anything in return.

How to serve without needing a spotlight.

How to love, deeply and deliberately.

She gave us her best—on the days when she was running on empty.

She gave us her best—when she had to choose between what she needed and what we did.

She gave us her best—when we didn't even know to ask.

And now that we are older, now that we carry responsibilities of our own, we look back and understand the weight she carried, and the beauty in how she carried it.

She gave us her best—because she believed we were worth it.

And now, every time we give our best to the people we love, every time we hold our heads high in adversity, every time we put someone else first, we honor her.

Because her best didn't just raise us—

It lives through us.

Chapter Reflection: She Gave Us Her Best

Scripture Reflection – KJV

"She looketh well to the ways of her household, and eateth not the bread of idleness."

— Proverbs 31:27

Reflection Prompt

Think about a time when your mother or a mother-figure gave you her best, even when you didn't know it at the time. What sacrifices have you come to recognize? How can you carry her spirit of giving into your own life and relationships?

Write your reflection below:

My Reflection

Chapter 18

The Table Still Stands

(The Place Where Legacy Was Served)

Long before we understood its meaning, she set the table.

Not just with plates, forks, and folded napkins—

but with values, discipline, warmth, and **presence.**

She made the table a place of rhythm and refuge.

A place where we learned how to pause.

How to listen.

How to speak with intention.

How to be grateful—regardless of how much or how little we had.

We thought we were just sitting down for dinner.

But we were being **formed**.

She fed us more than meals.

She fed us *morals*.

She served up wisdom between spoonfuls of food.

She dished out lessons with every side of patience and every helping of grace.

Her table was never just about eating—

It was about **gathering**, **growing**, and **grounding**.

We laughed at that table.

We were corrected at that table.

We prayed at that table.

And sometimes, we sat in silence, but her presence said more than words ever could.

We learned how to have hard conversations.

We learned how to make room for each other.

We learned what family meant—at that table.

It didn't matter if it was chicken and rice or leftovers from the night before—

When she set the table, we knew **love was being served.**

And now that she's no longer here to sit at the head,
now that her hands no longer stir the pots or call us to
come eat…

The table still stands.

Because it was never just about the food.

It was about the foundation.

It was about the structure she gave us when everything
else in life felt uncertain.

She built that table with sacrifice.

She protected it with consistency.

She anointed it with prayer.

She filled it with warmth that outlasts the seasons and the
sorrow.

That table was her altar.

That table was her classroom.

That table was her *gift*.

And even now, when the room is different…

When the voices are older…

When the chairs don't feel quite as full…

Her table still feeds us.

It feeds us every time we show up for one another.

It feeds us every time we hold space for someone hurting.

It feeds us every time we extend forgiveness across the table,

and every time we choose peace over pride.

The table still teaches.

The table still welcomes.

The table still calls us back to the center of who we are.

Because **she built it with more than wood—**

She built it with wisdom.

And now, as we carry on her traditions, as we prepare our own tables, as we speak to our children and invite others in—

we do so with her voice in our hearts and her spirit in the room.

The table she set is now the table we live by.

And as long as we honor what she built, as long as we pass down the love she laid out for us—

Her table will never fall.

Her table will never fade.

Her table still stands.

Chapter Reflection: The Table Still Stands

Scripture Reflection – KJV

"Wisdom hath builded her house, she hath hewn out her seven pillars: She hath killed her beasts; she hath mingled her wine; she hath also furnished her table."
— *Proverbs 9:1–2*

Reflection Prompt

What memories do you have of your mother setting a "table" of love, teaching, or tradition? How do you continue her legacy through your own table—whether spiritual, emotional, or physical?

Write your reflection below:

My Reflection

Chapter 19

Her Legacy Is Alive in Us

(What She Planted, We Now Carry)

Legacy is more than a memory.

It's more than a photograph or a story passed down.

It's more than a date etched in stone or a name spoken on anniversaries.

Legacy is alive.

And hers lives on—not just in what she left, but in what she **left within us**.

She didn't just leave behind possessions—

She left behind *principles*.

She didn't just raise children—

She planted leaders, caregivers, givers, believers.

Her legacy is not a moment frozen in time.

It's a fire that still burns.

It's a foundation that still holds.

It's a light that still guides.

We see her in our decisions.

In the way we think before we speak.

In the way we offer help without hesitation.

In the way we choose integrity over impulse, purpose over pride.

She taught us that love isn't always grand—it's faithful.

That showing up matters more than showing off.

That your name isn't just what you're called—

It's what you live up to.

And now, long after she's gone, her life still echoes in ours.

Her compassion still teaches us how to be gentle.

Her boldness still teaches us how to stand firm.

Her devotion still reminds us that being consistent is a form of love.

When we forgive quickly—she's there.

When we speak truth without cruelty—she's there.

When we carry ourselves with dignity, even in difficult moments—**she's there.**

She loved us in ways we didn't always understand at the time.

And now, with years and life behind us, we see that her way of loving was preparation.

She was laying the groundwork.

She was building legacy.

She was pouring into a future she knew she might not see—but believed in anyway.

That's the kind of love only a mother can give.

And that's the kind of legacy that can't die.

We carry her in our tone, in our timing, in our truthfulness.

We carry her when we lead with humility, when we choose what's right over what's easy, when we sacrifice quietly because someone else needs more.

She shaped us.

Not into perfection—but into **purpose.**

And now, every act of kindness, every moment of wisdom, every decision rooted in love and faith—
is a reflection of her.

She may not be here to witness the men we're becoming.

But we are becoming those men **because of her.**

Because of what she endured.

Because of what she taught.

Because of how she lived when no one was watching.

She left us a legacy that isn't measured in things—

It's measured in truth.

In faith.

In strength.

In presence.

And as long as we live, **her legacy will never die.**

Because what she started, **we now carry.**

Chapter Reflection: Her Legacy Is Alive in Us

Scripture Reflection – KJV

"The just man walketh in his integrity: his children are blessed after him."

— Proverbs 20:7

Reflection Prompt

In what ways is your mother or mother-figure's legacy alive in your daily life? How do your choices, values, and relationships reflect her presence and the lessons she left behind?

Write your reflection below:

My Reflection

Chapter 20

Roots of Honor: Standing on Her Shoulders

(What She Rooted, We Now Rise)

Honor is more than a lesson.

It's more than a rule carved in time.

It's more than a moment when she stood tall and spoke.

Honor is a living root.

And hers grows deep—not just in what she said, but in what she sowed within us.

She didn't just model courage—

She anchored conviction.

She didn't just teach right and wrong—

She planted unwavering truth, resilience, and grace.

Roots of honor don't shout—*they hold.*

They hold firm through winds of doubt,

When whispers of compromise tempt our resolve.

They hold firm through seasons of plenty,

When pride beckons with empty praise.

They hold firm through droughts of approval,

When the world's applause falls silent.

We feel her in our posture—

In the steady lift of our chin when fear would bow us.

We feel her in our *choices*—

In the silent vow to speak truth, even when silence seems easier.

We feel her in our hands—

Offering steadiness where chaos seeks to shake.

She didn't just pass down rules—

She passed down purpose.

In early dawn's soft glow, she rose to labor—

Teaching us that true service begins before recognition.

In nightly hush, she lingered in prayer—

Teaching us that our roots draw strength from faith.

When we hesitate before an unfair demand—

She's there in our conscience, *urging courage*.

When we pause before a hasty word—

She's there reminding us that integrity speaks in kindness.

When we stand alone for justice—

She's there in the quiet power that won't relent.

Honor grows in the soil of sacrifice.

We learned it when she set aside her own comfort,

Bearing burdens so we would not bend.

We felt it when she forgave our failures,

Tilling our guilt into lessons of redemption.

We witnessed it when she held her tongue against gossip,

Guarding our family's name with dignified restraint.

Roots of honor don't collapse under strain—

They deepen.

As storms of trial roll *overhead*,

Our roots entwine with hers, *unbreakable*.

As seasons of blessing rain upon us,

Our roots draw nourishment from her legacy.

She planted in us more than memory—

She planted life.

And now, each act of steadfastness,

Each choice of humility over hubris,

Each word spoken in truth and love,

Blooms because of what she rooted.

And when we falter—

She's there in our resolve to stand again.

When we succeed—

She's there in our gratitude that anchors our joy.

When we lead others—

She's there in the honor that guides our way.

Her roots live in our choices.

Her strength lives in our courage.

Her honor lives in our hearts.

As long as we walk the path she *paved*—

Her legacy of honor will rise in us,

Unseen beneath our steps,

Yet unyielding in every season.

Chapter Reflection: Roots of Honor - Standing on Her Shoulders

Scripture Reflection – KJV

"The just man walketh in his integrity: his children are blessed after him."

— Proverbs 20:7

Reflection Prompt

In what ways has your mother or mother-figure's unwavering integrity shaped the choices you make today? How do your actions and commitments reflect the roots of honor she planted within you?

Write your reflection below:

My Reflection:

Chapter 21

Hands That Held: The Power of Presence

Presence is more than an embrace.

It's more than a warm meal on a cold evening.

It's more than a whisper in the dark or a hand on a fevered brow.

Presence is faithful.

And hers remains constant—not just in the grand celebrations, but in the small moments she chose to arrive.

She didn't just offer *comfort*—

She offered *herself.*

She didn't just fill our days with activity—

She filled our hearts with assurance.

Presence doesn't demand *spotlight*—it simply *shows.*

It shows up in the rustle of footsteps outside a hospital door,

In the quiet hum of waiting through life's uncertainties.

It shows up in the soft murmur of bedtime stories,

In the unhurried patience of listening when words falter.

We *feel* her in our company—

In the way we pause our own agendas to listen.

We *feel* her in our timing—

In the gentle art of being there before being asked.

We *feel* her in our hands—

Ready to lift, to steady, to wipe away tears without drawing attention.

She didn't just schedule her presence—

She wove herself into our daily patterns.

In the dawn's stillness, she was there to guide our first steps—

Teaching us that *faithfulness* begins with the unseen acts.

In twilight's hush, she was there to close our eyes—

Teaching us that *love* lingers long after the day's demands.

When we hesitate to make a friend feel welcomed—

She's there in our courage to extend the invitation.

When we doubt whether our presence matters—

She's there in our choice to stay through the awkward silence.

When we see someone alone in need—

She's there in our hands reaching across the distance.

Presence is sacrifice woven into time.

We learned it when she set aside her own rest,

Sitting by our bedsides through restless nights.

We learned it when she answered our calls at odd hours,

Proving that love isn't *measured by convenience.*

We learned it when she paused her chores to cradle our worries,

Showing that to carry someone's pain is the highest form of care.

Hands that held don't let go at the first sign of struggle—

They hold firmer.

As life's burdens press upon us,

We bear them for each other as she bore ours.

As plans shift and dreams waver,

We remain steadfast, a lineage of faithful presence.

She planted in us more than memories—

She planted the legacy of arrival.

And now, each time we close the distance between sorrow and solace,

Each time we choose to linger a little longer,

Each time we let our footprints mark the path back to hope,

We honor what she carried in her hands.

And when we're needed—

We arrive.

When fear grips another—

We offer our quiet strength.

When the world rushes past—

We stand still, grounded in the promise that presence is love articulated.

Her *hands* live in our touch.

Her *faithfulness* lives in our footsteps.

Her *legacy* lives in the moments we simply stay.

As long as we choose to show up—

Her *power of presence* will echo on,

Unseen in the grand tally of time,

Yet felt in every heartbeat of care.

Chapter Reflection: Hands That Held: The Power of Presence

Scripture Reflection – KJV

"Bear ye one another's burdens, and so fulfill the law of Christ."

— Galatians 6:2

Reflection Prompt

In what moments have you offered faithful presence to someone in need? How does your availability and attentiveness mirror the quiet, constant love you received?

Write your reflection below:

My Reflection

Chapter 22

Words of Grace: Speaking Life into Others

Words of grace are more than polite phrases.

They're more than empty pleasantries or social niceties.

They're more than a compliment offered in passing.

Words of grace are living echoes.

And hers still resonate—not just in what she said, but in how she taught us to speak.

She didn't just *talk* to us—

She spoke life into us.

She didn't just *correct our errors*—

She offered gentle truth wrapped in kindness.

Graceful words don't shine—*they soothe.*

They soothe doubt when we hesitate at new beginnings.

They soothe shame when we stumble under our own weight.

They soothe fear when our hearts tremble with uncertainty.

We hear her in our *greetings*—

In the warmth we extend before expectation.

We hear her in our *apologies*—

In the sincerity that mends what we've broken.

We hear her in our *encouragement*—

In the faith we plant in another's trembling hope.

She didn't just teach us vocabulary—

She taught us virtue.

In her laughter, we learned that *joy softens hard days.*

In her pauses, we learned that *listening honors the speaker.*

In her questions, we learned that *curiosity invites growth.*

When we hesitate before speaking—

She's there in the gentle nudge toward honesty.

When we struggle to comfort a friend—

She's there in the kindness we offer without judgment.

When we seek the right words at the right time—

She's there in our memory of her patient voice.

Words of grace grow in the soil of empathy.

We learned it when she whispered reassurance on sleepless nights,

Turning tears into courage.

We felt it when she affirmed our dreams,

Transforming doubt into determination.

We witnessed it when she spoke truth to our faltering faith,

Guiding us back to our higher calling.

Speaking life is not about grand speeches—

It's about faithful phrases.

A single *"I believe in you"* can uplift more than a thousand cheers.

A simple *"I'm listening"* can heal more than elaborate counsel.

A heartfelt *"I'm sorry"* can restore more than a proud defense.

When our words bring comfort—

She's there in the love that flows through us.

When our words inspire action—

She's there in the courage we pass along.

When our words reveal truth—

She's there in the integrity that undergirds them.

She planted in us more than eloquence—

She planted compassion.

And now, each phrase of kindness,

Each confession of humility,

Each affirmation of another's worth,

Blooms because of what she whispered.

Her voice lives in our speech.

Her grace lives in our language.

Her love lives in every sentence we offer.

As long as we speak with gentle courage—

Her legacy of words of grace will echo in us,

Alive in every conversation,

Enriching every heart.

Chapter Reflection: Words of Grace: Speaking Life into Others

Scripture Reflection – KJV

"Pleasant words are as an honeycomb, sweet to the soul, and health to the bones."

— Proverbs 16:24

Reflection Prompt

How have the gentle words of your mother or mother-figure shaped the way you speak to others? In what situations do you most clearly hear her voice guiding your tone and choice of words?

Write your reflection below:

My Reflection:

Chapter 23

Gentle Fires: Passion Tempered by Patience

Passion is more than a spark.

It's more than a flash of brilliance or a moment of heat.

It's more than the blaze that dazzles and dies too soon.

Passion is a gentle fire.

And hers burned not to consume, but to cultivate—igniting dreams with mindful restraint.

She didn't just urge us to dream—

She taught us to steward those dreams with care.

She didn't just fan our flames—

She tempered our *zeal* with *compassion*, so our fires would warm without burning others.

Gentle fires don't roar—they glow.

They glow steadily through the night of uncertainty,

When doubt threatens to snuff out our hope.

They glow steadily through the winds of haste,

When impatience would scorch the fragile shoots of growth.

They glow steadily through storms of criticism,

When harsh words seek to extinguish our resolve.

We sense her in our *ambitions*—

In the way we dare greatly, yet pause to ensure our reach does not overshadow another's need.

We sense her in our *efforts*—

In the way we labor with intensity, yet stop to replenish weary hearts.

We sense her in our *achievements*—

In the way we celebrate success with humility, mindful of the hands that helped guide our fire.

She didn't just plant passion—

She planted purpose.

In the bright morning of our first victories, she remained our calm harbor—

Reminding us that every triumph carries responsibility.

In the dusk of our deepest failures, she lingered with a steady lamp—

Reminding us that *resilience* rises when hope is rekindled.

When ambition threatens to burn bridges—

She's there in the gentle pause, reminding us that relationships matter more than rapid ascent.

When zeal tempts us to bulldoze the vulnerable—

She's there in the soft whisper, teaching us that compassion fuels a fire that lasts.

When success dazzles with hollow acclaim—

She's there in the quiet counsel, guiding us back to humble service.

Patience is the soil where passion takes root.

We learned it when she delayed immediate gratification,

Choosing long-term growth over quick thrills.

We felt it when she held our hands through slow progress,

Turning small steps into steady strides.

We witnessed it when she forgave the misfires of our youthful fervor,

Transforming our mistakes into lessons of perseverance.

Gentle fires don't *flicker*—they *endure*.

As seasons of challenge descend,

Our fires burn on, buffered by her steady care.

As seasons of triumph rise,

Our fires burn on, warmed by her enduring love.

She ignited in us more than desire—

She ignited discipline.

And now, each act of bold kindness,

Each pursuit of dreams laced with empathy,

Each moment of steady determination,

Shines because of how she trained our flame.

And when our fervor wanes—

She's there in our resolve to reignite.

When our focus drifts—

She's there in our call back to deliberate action.

When our passion soars—

She's there in the compass of compassion that guides our glow.

Her fire lives in our *zeal*.

Her patience lives in our *pace*.

Her compassion lives in our *warmth*.

As long as we walk the path she illuminated—

Her gentle fire of passion tempered by **patience**

Will burn in us,

Visible in every dream pursued with care,

Unquenchable in every heart she taught to glow.

Chapter Reflection: Gentle Fires: Passion Tempered by Patience

Scripture Reflection – KJV

"Be ye fervent in spirit; serving the Lord."

— Romans 12:11

Reflection Prompt

In what areas of your life do you feel God-given passion burning? How might you temper that zeal with patience and compassion, ensuring your pursuits build up others rather than burn them?

Write your reflection below:

My Reflection:

Chapter 24

Seeds of Service: Planting Generosity

Generosity is more than a gift.

It's more than a coin placed in a hand.

It's more than applause for grand gestures.

Generosity is living seed.

And hers takes root—not just in what she gave, but in what she grew within us.

She didn't just open her purse—

She opened her heart.

She didn't just share her treasures—

She shared her time, her talent, her tenderness.

Seeds of service drift quietly through our days.

They settle in moments unnoticed:

A borrowed sweater for a shivering friend;

An unhurried ear for a weary soul;

A midnight car ride to a hospital bedside.

We *feel* her in those seeds—

A gentle whisper to give again,

Even when our own wells feel low.

We see her in each sprout of kindness—

A life coached by her example, *flourishing* in our hands.

She taught us that true service bends the proud back toward humility—

When she scrubbed floors before dawn, so we could dream without worry.

When she greeted strangers as kin, so we learned that *every face hides a story.*

When she lifted weary neighbors with warm meals, so we knew that *love feeds bodies and souls alike.*

Service is not a scoreboard—

It doesn't tally favors or demand recognition.

It's the quiet life-force of compassion.

It's mercy sowed among the thorny weeds of need.

When disappointment would harden our hearts—

She's there in the offering of a hand.

When *bitterness* threatens to take root—

She's there in the grace we scatter.

When despair whispers that nothing's worth giving—

She's there in our resolve to sow anyway.

Seeds of service flourish in sacrifice.

We learned it in the nights she stayed awake,

Rocking our worries into sleep.

We saw it in the days she set aside her comfort,

Answering the call of another's pain.

We felt it in the years she chose people over plans,

Attending birthdays, funerals, weddings—no invitation too small.

Service grows in community.

As her seeds took hold in us,

We watched them sprout in neighbors, friends, children—

A garden of generosity blooming beyond her sight.

And now, we carry trowel and watering can,

Tilling soil, scattering hope, trusting in the miracles of small offerings.

She planted in us more than compassion—

She planted purpose.

And now, every shared meal, every lifted burden, every silent prayer for someone else's joy,

Is a blossom of her *legacy*.

When we hesitate at the *doorstep* of need—

She's there in the courage to enter.

When we ration our resources—

She's there reminding us that abundance begins with a *willing* heart.

When we witness lack and turn away—

She's there in the stirring that calls us back.

Her *seeds* live in our *service*.

Her *love* lives in our *giving*.

Her *legacy* lives in our *harvest of blessing*.

As long as hands reach out, as long as hearts respond—

Her seeds of service will scatter through the world,

Invisible yet inexhaustible,

Rooted in her love and blooming in ours.

Chapter Reflection: Seeds of Service: Planting Generosity

Scripture Reflection – KJV

"Whoever is generous to the poor lends to the Lord, and he will repay him for his deed."

— Proverbs 19:17

Reflection Prompt

In what acts of service do you see your mother or mother-figure's generosity reflected? How has her example inspired you to give without expectation, and where might you plant new seeds of kindness today?

Write your reflection below:

My Reflection:

Chapter 25

Lamps of Wisdom: Light for Every Path

(What She Illuminated, We Now Carry)

Wisdom is more than knowledge.

It's more than advice spoken in a hurry.

It's more than a lofty quote or a clever proverb.

Wisdom is living light.

And hers still shines—not just in the words she spoke, but in the way she walked among us.

She didn't just offer *suggestions*—

She kindled understanding.

She didn't just talk of purpose—

She showed us how to seek it, step by careful step.

Lamps of wisdom don't glare—*they glow*.

They glow steady through confusion's fog,

When every choice seems shrouded in doubt.

They glow steady through disappointment's shadow,

When dreams flicker on the brink of extinguish.

They glow steady through triumph's glare,

When pride would *blind* us to what truly *matters*.

We see her at every *crossroads*—

A gentle *hand* lifting our lantern.

We hear her in every question—

A calm voice guiding toward deeper truth.

We feel her in every pause—

A patient presence teaching us to wait on clarity.

She didn't just plant seeds of insight—

She tended them with *patient* care.

In the hush of dawn, she listened—to her own heart, to our questions—

Teaching us that discernment begins in stillness.

In the glow of evening's lamp, she reflected—on choices made, on lessons learned—

Teaching us that purpose unfolds over time.

When we encounter paths that twist and fork—

She's there in our inner compass, pointing true north.

When we *wrestle* with decisions that weigh heavy—

She's there in the quiet counsel to lean on faith.

When we yearn for direction in barren seasons—

She's there in the unwavering flame that refuses to die.

Wisdom grows in the soil of experience.

We learned it when she shared both triumphs and missteps,

Bearing her own failures with *humility.*

We felt it when she invited questions,

Tilling our curiosity into understanding.

We *witnessed* it when she trusted us to decide,

Guiding our steps but never stealing our choice.

Lamps of wisdom don't flicker under trial—

They shine brighter.

As nights of uncertainty stretch long,

Our lamps burn with the fuel of her faith.

As days of clarity dawn,

Our lamps reflect the warmth of her example.

She *illuminated* more than paths—

She *illuminated* hearts.

And now, each moment of clear-eyed insight,

Each decision made with purpose,

Each act of discernment in love and truth,

Glows because of what she handed down.

And when shadows return—

She's there in our resolve to kindle light again.

When we *misstep*—

She's there in our return to honest reflection.

When we *guide others*—

She's there in the lamp we carry forward.

Her light lives in our choices.

Her wisdom lives in our hearts.

Her purpose lives in our steps.

As long as we walk the paths she lit—

Her *legacy* of wisdom will shine in us,

Unseen in the daylight,

Yet *unquenchable* in every season.

Chapter Reflection: Lamps of Wisdom: Light for Every Path

Scripture Reflection – KJV

"Thy word is a lamp unto my feet, and a light unto my path."

— Psalm 119:105

Reflection Prompt

In what situations have you sensed your mother or mother-figure's wisdom guiding you through uncertainty? How do you now carry her light into your own decisions and the paths you walk?

Write your reflection below:

My Reflection:

Chapter 26

Echoes of Forgiveness: Freedom in Letting Go

Forgiveness is more than an *apology*.

It's more than a pardon granted in words.

It's more than *erasing* a wrong from memory.

Forgiveness is a living echo.

And hers resonates—not just in the mercy she offered, but in the mercy she planted within us.

She didn't just excuse mistakes—

She released burdens.

She didn't just say *"I forgive you"*—

She taught us to forgive ourselves, to breathe again.

Echoes of forgiveness don't vanish—they reverberate.

They reverberate in the hush after confession,

When peace settles where guilt once festered.

They reverberate in the space between two hearts,

Where *walls* once stood tall.

They reverberate in our own tender words,

When we choose *compassion* over *condemnation*.

We feel her in our breath—

A quiet release when resentment tightens our chest.

We feel her in our embrace—

A *warmth* that bridges what anger tore apart.

We feel her in our voice—

Soft yet steady as we offer grace to others and to ourselves.

She didn't just show us *mercy*—

She modeled freedom.

In the gentle way she let go of past hurts,

She taught us that holding on only binds the soul.

In the *loving* way she welcomed repentance,

She taught us that true healing begins when we meet brokenness with kindness.

When we stumble under regret—

She's there in our courage to admit fault.

When we *tremble* before *mending* a fractured bond—

She's there in our *willingness* to reach out first.

When we tremble at forgiving the unforgivable—

She's there in the whisper of hope that love can conquer all.

Forgiveness grows in the soil of *vulnerability.*

We learned it when she bared her own wounds,

Admitting her imperfections so we could heal ours.

We felt it when she offered her hand without hesitation,

Inviting us to step into a new beginning.

We witnessed it when she refused to tally wrongs,

Choosing instead to sow seeds of reconciliation.

Echoes of forgiveness don't fade—they deepen.

As years stretch onward,

Our own acts of mercy become testimony to hers.

As new offenses arise,

Our capacity to let go expands, nourished by her example.

She *planted* in us more than release—

She planted restoration.

And now, each time we choose peace over pride,

Each time we whisper *"I forgive,"*

Each time we offer *grace* before justice,

We carry her *echoes* into every tomorrow.

Chapter Reflection: Echoes of Forgiveness: Freedom in Letting Go

Scripture Reflection – KJV

"And be ye kind one to another, tenderhearted, forgiving one another, even as God for Christ's sake hath forgiven you."

— Ephesians 4:32

Reflection Prompt

Reflect on a time when you extended or received forgiveness. How did that act of mercy reshape your heart and relationships? In what ways can you carry forward the freedom found in letting go?

Write your reflection below:

My Reflection:

Chapter 27

Quiet Sacrifices: The Strength of Surrender

(What She Gave, We Now Guard)

Sacrifice is more than a forfeit.

It's more than a cost counted in sleep lost or tears shed.

It's more than quiet deeds unseen by the world.

Sacrifice is a choice alive.

And hers lives on—not in what she lost, but in what she gained for us.

She didn't just give her time—

She poured out her own comfort.

She didn't just offer help—

She surrendered her own desires for another's need.

Quiet sacrifices don't demand applause—they *endure*.

They endure in midnight vigils beside a fevered brow,

When she *whispered prayers* into the hush of the room.

They endure in lunches skipped so we could learn,

When empty plates marked lessons of priority.

They endure in tears held back, dignity intact,

When her heart broke at our failures, yet she offered grace.

We feel her in our *readiness to* yield—

In the gentle step aside so someone else may pass.

We feel her in our willingness to wait—

When our dreams must pause for another's healing.

We feel her in our humility to bend—

For the sake of mending fractured trust.

She didn't just show us strength—

She taught us surrender.

In the silent strength of her bowed head,

She revealed that letting go can be the greatest hold.

In the measured grace of her unspoken "no,"

She revealed that boundaries *protect* more than they confine.

When we choose the harder path of service—

She's there in the echo of her steady hands.

When we lay down prizes for someone else's gain—

She's there in the calm of our released grip.

When we stay present through *discomfort*—

She's there in the *courage* that blooms within our hearts.

Strength of surrender grows in the soil of trust.

We learned it when she *entrusted* our broken bits

Into the hands of forgiveness, sealing us with hope.

We felt it when she laid aside her wounded pride

So we might learn compassion before judgment.

We witnessed it when she chose peace over vindication,

Teaching us that *unity* often demands personal yield.

Quiet sacrifices don't fade—they multiply.

As we pass her example through each selfless act,

Our own hands become vessels for her love.

As we comfort the weary, feed the hungry,

Our hearts carry forward the legacy of her giving.

She *planted* in us more than gratitude—

She planted resolve.

And now, every surrendered comfort,

Every unseen kindness,

Every gentle boundary set for another's good,

Blooms because of what she gave.

And when we hesitate—

She's there in our renewed resolve to serve.

When we falter under pressure—

She's there in our vow to stand again.

When we offer up our will for a higher cause—

She's there in the strength that holds us fast.

Her *sacrifice* lives in our compassion.

Her surrender lives in our strength.

Her love lives in our giving.

As long as we choose others' needs over our own—

Her *legacy* of quiet sacrifice will endure,

Unheralded yet unbreakable,

A testament to the *strength* of surrender.

Chapter Reflection: Quiet Sacrifices: The Strength of Surrender

Scripture Reflection – KJV

"Bear ye one another's burdens, and so fulfil the law of Christ."

— Galatians 6:2

Reflection Prompt

In what ways have you witnessed or practiced quiet sacrifice in your own life? How does choosing to surrender your comfort for another's need reflect the legacy of your mother or mother-figure?

Write your reflection below:

My Reflection:

Chapter 28

Bridge Builders: Uniting Hearts with Humility

Reconciliation is more than agreement.

It's more than polite conversation or shared laughter.

It's more than a handshake across a table.

Reconciliation is alive.

And hers lives on—not just in the peacemaking she did, but in the peacemakers she raised.

She didn't just preach forgiveness—

She practiced it.

She didn't just encourage *unity*—

She embodied humility, leaning in where walls once stood.

Humility doesn't acquiesce—*it invites.*

It invites a listening ear when anger roars.

It invites a gentle word when pride heats the heart.

It invites a shared meal when distance grows wide.

We see her in the way we draw near to hurt.

In the way we speak softly into tension.

In the way we choose understanding over defense, empathy over ego.

She taught us that courage isn't always about standing tall—*it's about bending low*.

That healing isn't always a grand gesture—it's faithful presence.

That true strength isn't loud—it's quiet enough to hear another's pain.

She built *bridges* in moments no one noticed.

At kitchen tables where arguments threatened to bloom,

She poured out tea with a smile,

Turning hot words into cooled reflection.

In living rooms where old wounds throbbed,

She offered her shoulder to cry on,

Turning distance into shared heartbeat.

When we confront our own grudges—

She's there in our whispered prayer for grace.

When we hesitate before extending olive branches—

She's there in the memory of her first step toward us.

When we listen deeply to someone we've wronged—

She's there in the patience she gave us when we were wrong.

Bridge building grows from humble soil.

We learned it when she admitted her own mistakes,

Turning confession into connection.

We felt it when she sought forgiveness for unintended hurt,

Showing us that apology is the sweetest key.

We witnessed it when she lifted others' dignity above her own,

Proving that *humility* is the highest door to unity.

Bridges aren't built in a day—they rise beam by beam.

With every act of listening,

With every choice to yield,

With every moment we place another's needs beside our own,

We carry on her work.

She planted in us more than peaceable seeds—

She planted bridge builders.

And now, each tender word,

Each patient pause,

Each humble act of service,

Spans the gaps she taught us to *heal*.

And when walls surround us—

She's there in our courage to dismantle them.

When voices harden—

She's there in our soft reply.

When unity seems *distant*—

She's there in our vision of a shared horizon.

Her bridges live in our actions.

Her unity lives in our hearts.

Her humility lives in our *hands*.

As long as we span divides with gentle strength—

Her legacy of bridge building will bind us,

Unseen yet unbroken,

And because of what she *bridged*, we now belong.

Chapter Reflection: Bridge Builders: Uniting Hearts with Humility

Scripture Reflection – KJV

"Behold, how good and how pleasant it is for brethren to dwell together in unity."

— Psalm 133:1

Reflection Prompt

In what situations has your mother or mother-figure modeled humility to bring healing or unity? How do your own efforts at reconciliation reflect the bridges she built?

Write your reflection below:

My Reflection:

Chapter 29

Everlasting Flame: Passing the Torch Forward

(What She Kindled, We Now Ignite)

Legacy is more than what we inherit.

It's more than the stories we recount.

It's more than the gratitude we voice today.

Legacy is a living flame.

And hers still burns—not just in what she began, but in what she entrusted to our hands.

She didn't just show us how to shine—

She taught us how to light others.

She didn't just spark our first steps—

She instilled in us the courage to carry fire into dark places.

An everlasting flame doesn't flicker—it endures.

It endures through the night of doubt,

When hope seems faint.

It endures through winds of change,

When the future feels uncertain.

It endures through the chill of fear,

When our hearts threaten to grow cold.

We feel her in our vision—

In the boldness to dream beyond what we can see.

We feel her in our hands—

Extending warmth where there is need.

We feel her in our words—

Sharing light through encouragement and truth.

She didn't just ignite our passion—

She entrusted us with the spark for generations yet unseen.

In every act of mentorship, she whispered: "Pass it on."

In every gift of time, she demonstrated: "Invest it wisely."

In every sacrificial moment, she declared: "Light costs something—but it's worth the price."

When we offer kindness to strangers—

She's there in our compassion's glow.

When we stand for justice in silent rooms—

She's there in our unwavering resolve.

When we nurture a child's curiosity—

She's there in the spark that kindled their wonder.

Passing the torch forward is not a single act—

It's a lifetime of choices.

We carry her flame when we speak courage to the fainthearted,

When we build bridges where there were walls,

When we lift voices that have been silenced.

Her flame lives in our generosity—

In the moments we give without remembering.

Her flame lives in our mercy—

In the forgiveness we extend before blame is earned.

Her flame lives in our vision—

In the futures we dare to imagine because she did.

An everlasting flame doesn't die at our own end—

It leaps from hand to waiting hand,

Igniting hope in places we may never see.

And that's faith: believing the fire will burn on,

Long after we have gone.

She sowed embers of love, sacrifice, and courage.

And now it is our turn to nurture them.

To shield them from the winds of apathy,

To feed them with deeds of service,

To shield them in nights of despair.

When we gather with friends around new sparks—

She's there in our joyful warmth.

When we teach with patience and purpose—

She's there in our guiding flame.

When we step into unknown paths—

She's there lighting every footfall.

Her torch lives in our hands.

Her vision lives in our hearts.

Her flame lives in our deeds.

As long as we carry forward what she kindled—

Her legacy will blaze eternal,

A fire passed from our lives into the lives of all who follow.

Chapter Reflection: Everlasting Flame: Passing the Torch Forward

Scripture Reflection – KJV

"Whoever brings blessing will be enriched, and one who waters will himself be watered."

— Proverbs 11:25

Reflection Prompt

In what ways are you passing the torch of your mother or mother-figure's legacy into the next generation? How do your acts of service, mentorship, and faith keep her flame burning bright?

Write your reflection below:

My Reflection:

Chapter 30

Echoes of Grace: Finding Mercy in Our Mistakes

(What She Forgave, We Now Extend)

Grace is more than pardon.

It's more than an apology accepted.

It's more than a second chance offered.

Grace is an echo—

A gentle rebound of mercy that ripples through our lives.

And hers still resonates—not just in the forgiveness she gave, but in what she taught us to forgive within ourselves and others.

She didn't just say *"I forgive you"*—

She showed us how to forgive.

She didn't just soften her words—

She softened our hearts toward compassion.

Grace doesn't demand—**it releases.**

It releases the weight of regret,

When our missteps haunt our reflections.

It releases the sting of criticism,

When harsh judgments threaten our spirit.

It releases the fear of shame,

When past failures threaten to define us.

We hear her in our confession—

A quiet courage to name our faults without shame.

We feel her in our embrace—

An open arms that welcomes *brokenness* home.

We see her in our eyes—

The willingness to look past error and see the person beneath.

She didn't just speak mercy—

She lived it.

In every moment she let go of resentment,

She planted seeds of renewed hope.

In every time she offered grace instead of blame,

She taught us the freedom of forgiving.

When we stumble in pride—

She's there in our heart, urging humility.

When we lash out in anger—

She's there reminding us that love heals more than retribution.

When we shrink in self-doubt—

She's there pressing us to rise in self-compassion.

Grace grows in the soil of vulnerability.

We learned it when she admitted her own mistakes—

Owning her faults with courage,

So we would learn to own ours.

We felt it when she forgave us quickly—

Holding us through tears,

Transforming our shame into a teachable moment.

We witnessed it when she spoke kindly of those who hurt her—

Modelling the higher path of mercy.

Echoes of grace don't fade—**they grow louder.**

As we extend forgiveness,

Our own scars become stepping-stones for others.

As we spare the rod of harsh judgment,

Our words become bridges instead of barriers.

As we release the chains of resentment,

Our hearts become freer to love more deeply.

She planted grace in our souls,

And now it is our calling to amplify that echo.

To forgive the friend who let us down,

To speak gently to the one who wronged us,

To show compassion to ourselves in our own *failings*.

When we offer mercy to the undeserving—

She's there in our bold kindness.

When we serve without condition—

She's there in our liberated love.

When we accept our own imperfections—

She's there in our growing grace.

Her echo lives in our mercy.

Her echo lives in our healing.

Her echo lives in every act of forgiveness.

As long as we carry her grace forward—

Her legacy will reverberate through generations,

A living echo of mercy that never fades.

Chapter Reflection: Echoes of Grace: Finding Mercy in Our Mistakes

Scripture Reflection – KJV

"Be ye kind one to another, tenderhearted, forgiving one another, even as God for Christ's sake hath forgiven you."

— Ephesians 4:32

Reflection Prompt

In what ways has your mother or mother-figure's example of mercy shaped the way you forgive yourself and others? How do you let her gracious echo guide your responses to mistakes and misunderstandings?

Write your reflection below:

My Reflection:

Chapter 31

Wells of Wisdom: Drawing Deep from Her Counsel

(What She Whispered, We Now Drink)

Wisdom is more than *knowledge.*

It's more than advice neatly offered.

It's more than words delivered in a moment of need.

Wisdom is a well—

A quiet source that sustains when life runs *dry.*

And hers still flows—not just in what she taught, but in what she shaped within our hearts.

She didn't just speak truths—

She lived them.

She didn't just share counsel—

She created capacity to understand.

Wells of wisdom don't gush—**they whisper.**

They whisper in moments of uncertainty,

When the path ahead seems blurred.

They whisper in seasons of decision,

When our hearts yearn for direction.

They whisper in times of silence,

When the loudest voices drown within.

We feel her in our listening—

In the patient pause before we answer.

We feel her in our questions—

In the gentle probe that seeks depth, not surface.

We feel her in our silence—

In the space we hold for others to speak their truth.

She didn't just pass down lessons—

She passed down discernment.

In quiet evenings by lamplight, she shared her stories—

Each one a testament to faith tested, choices weighed.

In tender moments over tea's steam, she guided our minds—

Teaching that true wisdom blooms where humility and curiosity meet.

When we face a choice that tempts our comfort—

She's there in our conscience, reminding us to seek counsel.

When we rush to judgment in anger—

She's there in our heart, whispering patience.

When we long for quick answers—

She's there urging us to draw deeper.

Wisdom grows in the soil of humility.

We learned it when she admitted she didn't have all the answers—

Yet trusted God to guide her steps,

So we could learn to trust beyond our own understanding.

We felt it when she welcomed questions—

No matter how simple or profound,

Turning curiosity into a bridge toward truth.

We witnessed it when she spoke gently of others—

Balancing honesty with kindness,

Showing that wisdom honors both fact and feeling.

Wells of wisdom don't run dry—they replenish.

As we share her counsel,

Our words become refreshment for thirsty souls.

As we listen more than we speak,

Our hearts become reservoirs of understanding.

As we seek truth with open minds,

Our spirits become deeper, fuller wells.

She planted in us more than knowledge—

She planted insight.

And now, each act of patient listening,

Each question asked with genuine care,

Each truth spoken in love,

Overflow because of what she nurtured.

And when we guide others—

She's there in our gentleness.

When we mentor with compassion—

She's there in our clarity.

When we admit our own learning—

She's there in our humility.

Her well lives in our counsel.

Her depth lives in our hearts.

Her whispers live in every word of guidance.

As long as we draw deeply from what she shared—

Her legacy will sustain us and those we lead,

A living spring of wisdom that never falters.

Chapter Reflection: Wells of Wisdom: Drawing Deep from Her Counsel

Scripture Reflection – KJV

"Wisdom is the principal thing; therefore get wisdom: and with all thy getting get understanding."

— Proverbs 4:7

Reflection Prompt

In what ways do you draw upon the guidance your mother or mother-figure gave you when you face challenges? How do you balance listening and speaking to let her well of wisdom flow through your life?

Write your reflection below:

My Reflection:

Chapter 32

Handwritten Promises: Keeping Her Commitments Alive

(What She Promised, We Now Protect)

A promise is more than a word spoken.

It's more than an agreement made.

It's more than a handshake, a nod, a vow.

A promise is a covenant.

A quiet contract sealed by faithfulness,

A thread woven through trust,

A bond not easily broken.

And hers still holds—not just in what she pledged, but in what she lived.

She didn't just make promises—

She kept them.

She didn't just speak of loyalty—

She embodied it.

Handwritten promises don't fade—they deepen.

They deepen when seasons change,

When storms make keeping them harder than making them.

They deepen when the cost is higher than expected,

When sacrifice is required to stay true.

They deepen in the unseen places,

Where no applause rewards the effort.

We see her in our perseverance—

In the way we honor our word when it's inconvenient.

We feel her in our loyalty—

In the way we stand by those we love even when it's hard.

We hear her in our resolve—

In the whisper that says, "Keep going, even when no one sees."

She didn't just teach us to make promises—

She showed us how to live them.

In the small things—

The rides to practice, the late-night talks, the meals on weary nights.

In the sacred things—

The prayers over our heads, the sacrifices never spoken aloud.

When we want to quit—

She's there in our perseverance.

When we're tempted to back out—

She's there in our integrity.

When we wonder if it's worth it—

She's there reminding us that keeping our word is its own reward.

Promises are forged in the fires of testing.

We learned this when she stayed faithful even when it hurt.

We saw it when she fulfilled her commitments with tired hands but steady heart.

We witnessed it when she loved without expiration dates,

When she served without seeking return,

When she forgave without holding onto offense.

Handwritten promises don't gather dust—they gather strength.

As we fulfill what we've committed,

Our spirits are strengthened.

As we protect our word like treasure,

Our lives become testimonies.

As we choose faithfulness over convenience,

We echo her legacy.

She planted in us more than responsibility—

She planted loyalty.

And now, each promise kept,

Each word honored,

Each act of steadfast love,

Is a living signature of her on our hearts.

When we show up after everyone else has left—

She's there in our faithfulness.

When we keep our vows in silence—

She's there in our perseverance.

When we love through every season—

She's there in our legacy.

Her promises live in our commitments.

Her faithfulness lives in our endurance.

Her spirit lives in every promise we now keep.

As long as we walk in the vows she showed us how to honor—

Her legacy will remain unbroken,

A living testament to promises fulfilled with love.

Chapter Reflection: Handwritten Promises: Keeping Her Commitments Alive

Scripture Reflection – KJV

"Better is it that thou shouldest not vow, than that thou shouldest vow and not pay."

— Ecclesiastes 5:5

Reflection Prompt

In what ways has your mother or mother-figure's faithfulness to her promises shaped how you view commitment today? How do you honor her example in the way you keep your word?

Write your reflection below:

My Reflection:

Chapter 33

Songs in the Night: Her Melody Still Plays

A song is more than melody.

It's more than words strung together.

It's more than a tune hummed in passing.

A song is a lifeline.

It's a balm for brokenness,

A bridge across sorrow,

A light in the midnight hour.

And hers still plays—not just in what she sang, but in what she believed while she sang.

She didn't just sing hymns—

She lived them.

She didn't just raise her voice—

She raised hope.

Songs in the night don't fade—**they strengthen.**

They strengthen when tears fall harder than *rain.*

They strengthen when silence surrounds and answers seem far.

They strengthen when darkness lingers longer than expected.

We hear her in the melodies of our minds—

In the songs that rise up without warning.

We feel her in the rhythm of our hearts—

In the steady drumbeat of resilience.

We carry her in the harmony of hope—

In the way we find music even in our mourning.

She didn't just teach us to sing—

She taught us to worship.

In the valley and on the mountaintop,

In abundance and in need,

In laughter and in lament.

When grief threatens to silence us—

She's there in our praise.

When burdens grow too heavy—

She's there in our lifting of hands.

When joy seems impossible—

She's there in the quiet hum of trust.

Songs are born in the places of deepest need.

We learned it when we saw her sing in sorrow—

Lifting melodies as weapons against despair.

We learned it when we heard her hum in hope—

Stitching together broken moments with praise.

We learned it when she taught us that sometimes,

The greatest victories are sung before they are seen.

Songs in the night don't disappear—**they become legacy.**

As we sing through the struggles,

Our spirits grow stronger.

As we praise in the waiting,

Our faith stretches wider.

As we worship without seeing,

Our trust deepens beyond what the eye can measure.

She planted in us more than music—

She planted perseverance.

And now, every time a melody rises in our sorrow,

Every time a lyric reminds us to believe,

Every time worship flows even when words fail,

It is her legacy alive in us.

When we choose hope over despair—

She's there in our song.

When we choose faith over fear—

She's there in our anthem.

When we choose gratitude over grumbling—

She's there in our melody.

Her songs live in our hearts.

Her faith lives in our voice.

Her hope lives in every note we dare to sing.

As long as we lift songs in the dark,

Her melody will never cease,

A living chorus of faith, hope, and love.

Chapter Reflection: Songs in the Night: Her Melody Still Plays

Scripture Reflection – KJV

"And at midnight Paul and Silas prayed, and sang praises unto God: and the prisoners heard them."

— *Acts 16:25*

Reflection Prompt

In what ways have the songs, prayers, or words of your mother or mother-figure sustained you during difficult times? How do you carry her melody of faith into your own moments of darkness?

Write your reflection below:

My Reflection:

Chapter 34

Shelters of Grace: How She Covered Us

Grace is more than a gift.

It's more than a second chance.

It's more than mercy offered when it's undeserved.

Grace is a shelter.

A refuge from judgment,

A covering against shame,

A safe place to heal and begin again.

And hers still shelters us—*not just in what she gave, but in how she gave it.*

She didn't just cover us—

She protected us.

She didn't just forgive—

She restored.

Shelters of grace don't collapse—**they endure.**

They endure when we fail.

They endure when we fall short.

They endure when we're too broken to fix ourselves.

We feel her covering in our quiet recoveries—

In the second chances we now offer others.

We hear her voice in our gentle corrections—

In the way we lift instead of tear down.

We see her *reflection* in our patient love—

In the way we hold space for others to grow.

She didn't just show us grace—

She made it a home for us.

A place where mistakes weren't final.

A place where love wasn't earned but given.

A place where belonging wasn't conditional but constant.

When we choose forgiveness instead of *fury*—

She's there in our compassion.

When we choose patience instead of *punishment*—

She's there in our understanding.

When we choose grace over *judgment*—

She's there, steady as ever.

Grace is strongest when it is hardest to give.

We learned this when she loved us at our worst.

We learned this when she spoke life over us when we spoke *carelessly.*

We learned this when she saw past what we did wrong and reminded us who we still were.

Shelters of grace don't just protect—**they empower.**

As we give what we have received,

We build what she built.

As we extend mercy where it's needed most,

We plant seeds of healing.

As we cover others with love instead of condemnation,

We create legacies that ripple into generations.

She planted in us more than *kindness*—

She planted restoration.

And now, every moment we choose to mend instead of break,

Every word we choose to heal instead of harm,

Every heart we choose to welcome instead of judge,

Is another *shelter* of grace we build in her name.

When we forgive without conditions—

She's there in our spirit.

When we love without limits—

She's there in our hearts.

When we hope without hesitation—

She's there, still covering us with grace.

Her shelter lives in our choices.

Her grace lives in our reach.

Her legacy lives in every hand extended in mercy.

As long as we offer what she once offered us,

Her shelter will never fall,

A living sanctuary of love and grace.

Chapter Reflection: Shelters of Grace: How She Covered Us

Scripture Reflection – KJV

"And above all things have fervent charity among yourselves: for charity shall cover the multitude of sins."

— *1 Peter 4:8*

Reflection Prompt

In what ways has your mother or mother-figure's grace shaped how you treat others? How are you building shelters of grace in your relationships today?

Write your reflection below:

My Reflection:

Chapter 35

Bridges of Faith: Crossing Because She Believed

(What She Believed, We Now Walk Upon)

Faith is more than hope.

It's more than wishful thinking.

It's more than a dream whispered into the dark.

Faith is a bridge.

A crossing over fear,

A way across uncertainty,

A path carved through impossibility.

And hers still carries us—not just in what she believed, but in how she believed for us.

She didn't just have faith—

She fought for it.

She didn't just pray prayers—

She paved pathways.

Bridges of faith don't crumble—**they endure**.

They endure through storms of doubt.

They endure through winds of fear.

They endure through floods of failure.

We walk her bridges every day—

In the decisions we make when we don't have all the answers.

In the risks we take when the outcome is unclear.

In the trust we offer when nothing seems certain.

She didn't just show us faith when life was easy—

She showed us how to believe when everything said otherwise.

She showed us how to hope when the world gave no reason.

She showed us how to stand when standing seemed impossible.

When we pray bold prayers—

She's there in our courage.

When we dream bigger dreams—

She's there in our vision.

When we trust God's promises even in the waiting—

She's there, steady as ever.

Faith is strongest when it faces resistance.

We learned this from her trembling prayers whispered late at night.

We learned this from her steady words when fear loomed heavy.

We learned this from her unwavering hope that reached further than her own lifetime.

Bridges of faith don't just carry one generation—they carry many.

As we step forward in obedience,

We walk further than she could see.

As we trust in the unseen,

We build new crossings for those who come after.

As we believe beyond what is safe,

We turn her faith into future foundations.

She planted in us more than belief—

She planted boldness.

And now, every time we choose to move forward despite fear,

Every time we choose to trust the unseen Hand guiding us,

Every time we step out when staying would be easier,

We walk a little further on the bridge she built.

When we dare greatly—

She's there in our steps.

When we endure quietly—

She's there in our strength.

When we build what others said was impossible—

She's there, cheering us on still.

Her faith lives in our journey.

Her belief lives in our bravery.

Her legacy lives in every bridge we dare to cross.

As long as we keep walking forward,

Her faith will never fade,

A living testament to the God she trusted with everything.

Chapter Reflection: Bridges of Faith: Crossing Because She Believed

Scripture Reflection – KJV

"For we walk by faith, not by sight."

— 2 Corinthians 5:7

Reflection Prompt

What bridges of faith did your mother or mother-figure build for you? How are you continuing her walk of faith today, especially when the road is uncertain?

Write your reflection below:

My Reflection:

Chapter 36

Gardens of Patience: Growing What She Planted

Patience is more than waiting.

It's more than sitting still.

It's more than enduring time.

Patience is a garden.

A place where hope is sown,

Where faith is watered,

Where dreams are grown in the unseen places.

And her garden still blooms—not just in what she planted, but in how she tended us.

She didn't just wait—

She worked while waiting.

She didn't just endure—

She encouraged.

Gardens of patience don't wilt in the heat—they deepen their roots.

They deepen when promises seem delayed.

They deepen when prayers seem unanswered.

They deepen when growth is slow and hidden.

We tend her garden every day—

In the way we nurture what others might abandon.

In the way we persevere when results don't come quickly.

In the way we believe in small beginnings.

She didn't just plant seeds and walk away—

She stayed.

Through every season.

Through drought and storm.

Through barren soil and unseen progress.

When we choose to wait with hope—

She's there in our steadiness.

When we choose to believe through dry seasons—

She's there in our persistence.

When we choose to keep watering dreams no one else sees—

She's there, faithfully gardening within us.

Patience is strongest when impatience would be easier.

We learned this from her steady hands pulling weeds no one else noticed.

We learned this from her tireless faith in what couldn't yet be seen.

We learned this from her joy in the process, not just the harvest.

Gardens of patience don't just feed today—they nourish generations.

As we nurture what's been entrusted to us,

We extend her garden's borders.

As we protect tender shoots of hope,

We shelter what she once shielded.

As we delight in slow but sure growth,

We honor the way she loved.

She planted in us more than endurance—

She planted expectation.

And now, every time we nurture what takes time,

Every time we believe in what's not yet visible,

Every time we stay when others would leave,

We grow the garden she started.

When we sow kindness without needing immediate return—

She's there in our heart.

When we love without a deadline—

She's there in our spirit.

When we trust the process even when it's painful—

She's there, watering our faith.

Her patience lives in our growth.

Her love lives in our nurturing.

Her legacy lives in every seed we refuse to abandon.

As long as we tend what she planted,

Her garden will never wither,

A living testament to faithfulness in every season.

Chapter Reflection: Gardens of Patience: Growing What She Planted

Scripture Reflection – KJV

"And let us not be weary in well doing: for in due season we shall reap, if we faint not."

— Galatians 6:9

Reflection Prompt

What seeds of patience did your mother or mother-figure plant in you? How are you tending those seeds in your life today, even when the growth is slow?

Write your reflection below:

My Reflection:

Chapter 37

Songs in the Silence: Lessons She Taught Without Words

Wisdom is more than words.

It's more than lessons spoken aloud.

It's more than lectures or long conversations.

Wisdom is a melody.

A song sung in silence,

A truth lived without needing to be declared,

A life that teaches louder than any speech.

And her melody still plays—not just in what she said, but in how she lived.

She didn't just speak wisdom—

She embodied it.

She didn't just give advice—

She lived a life worth following.

Songs in the silence don't fade—**they echo**.

They echo in quiet choices made well.

They echo in gentle sacrifices unseen by many.

They echo in simple acts of love too deep for words.

We hear her song every day—

In the patience we offer without needing praise.

In the kindness we extend without needing recognition.

In the decisions we make when no one is watching.

She didn't teach us by demanding—

She taught us by doing.

She didn't shape us through noise—

She shaped us through presence.

Through her steady consistency.

Through her everyday example.

When we choose humility over attention—

She's there in our posture.

When we choose grace over anger—

She's there in our response.

When we choose perseverance over quitting—

She's there, singing softly in our spirit.

The loudest lessons are often the ones lived quietly.

We learned this from her silent prayers offered when no one listened.

We learned this from her steady strength when life was heavy.

We learned this from her faithfulness that didn't need to be noticed to be real.

Songs in the silence don't just instruct—they inspire.

As we live by her example,

We carry her melody forward.

As we choose integrity in small things,

We honor her song.

As we quietly pour love into others,

We join her silent choir.

She planted in us more than knowledge—

She planted character.

And now, every time we love without announcement,

Every time we serve without applause,

Every time we stand firm without needing affirmation,

We hear her song anew.

When we wait without complaint—

She's there in our spirit.

When we hope without demanding proof—

She's there in our soul.

When we live with honor in a world chasing attention—

She's there, humming a melody of grace.

Her wisdom lives in our silence.

Her faithfulness lives in our actions.

Her legacy lives in every quiet decision rooted in love.

As long as we remember her silent songs,

Her voice will never be forgotten,

A living testament to the power of a life well-lived without a word.

Chapter Reflection: Songs in the Silence: Lessons She Taught Without Words

Scripture Reflection – KJV

"Even so the tongue is a little member, and boasteth great things. Behold, how great a matter a little fire kindleth!"

— James 3:5

Reflection Prompt

What silent lessons did your mother or mother-figure teach you through her actions? How are you living out her quiet wisdom today?

Write your reflection below:

My Reflection:

____

____

____

____

Chapter 38

The Weight of Her Prayers: Covered by Her Faith

(What She Prayed For, We Now Walk In)

Prayer is more than words whispered into the dark.

It's more than folded hands and bowed heads.

It's more than a ritual done out of routine.

Prayer is a covering.

A shelter built out of belief.

A wall of hope stacked stone by stone.

And her prayers still cover us—not just in memory, but in movement.

She didn't just pray for outcomes—

She prayed for endurance.

She didn't just pray for blessings—

She prayed for becoming.

The weight of her prayers is not a burden—it's a blessing.

A blessing that shields us when life storms rage.

A blessing that lifts us when we falter.

A blessing that steadies us when the ground beneath us shakes.

We walk under her prayers every day—

In the doors that open we didn't knock on.

In the dangers avoided we didn't even see.

In the strength that shows up just when we need it most.

She didn't just ask God for things—

She asked God to shape us.

She asked Him to guide our steps.

To guard our hearts.

To build in us a resilience deeper than hardship.

When we find peace in chaos—

She's there in the prayers that went before us.

When we stand strong though we feel weak—

She's there in the petitions she lifted.

When we succeed beyond what we deserve—

She's there, having knelt in our place long before we arrived.

Prayer is the unseen work of love.

We learned this from her tear-stained nights.

We learned this from her whispered hopes over our sleeping heads.

We learned this from her unwavering belief even when circumstances gave no reason.

The weight of her prayers doesn't crush—it carries.

As we step into our calling,

We are walking on ground she covered.

As we overcome battles we didn't know she fought in prayer,

We carry her faith forward.

As we become who she dreamed we could be,

We fulfill promises she trusted God to keep.

She gave us more than protection—

She gave us provision.

And now, every time we trust instead of fear,

Every time we seek God before seeking solutions,

Every time we kneel in prayer for the next generation,

We join her lifelong labor.

When we pray over others with fierce tenderness—

She's there in our spirit.

When we believe for impossible things—

She's there in our heart.

When we stand with heaven's authority though our hands
are trembling—

She's there, her prayers still breathing life into ours.

Her faith lives in our courage.

Her hope lives in our perseverance.

Her love lives in every whispered prayer we now send up.

As long as we pray,

Her covering will never fall away,

A living testament to the love that fights on its knees.

Chapter Reflection: The Weight of Her Prayers: Covered by Her Faith

Scripture Reflection – KJV

"The effectual fervent prayer of a righteous man availeth much."

— James 5:16

Reflection Prompt

What prayers do you believe your mother or mother-figure prayed over you? How do you see the evidence of those prayers in your life today?

Write your reflection below:

My Reflection:

Chapter 39

The Gift of Her Grit: Endurance We Inherited

(What She Carried, We Now Continue)

Strength is more than muscle.

It's more than a loud roar or a lifted weight.

It's more than winning battles in the open.

Strength is quiet endurance.

It's standing firm when everything else crumbles.

It's pressing on when there's no applause.

And her strength still fuels us—not just in what she said, but in how she lived.

She didn't just survive hardships—

She overcame them with grace.

She didn't just carry burdens—

She carried them without losing her kindness.

The gift of her grit isn't loud—it's lasting.

It echoes in moments when we feel too weak to continue.

It anchors us when everything inside us wants to give up.

It whispers to us when the world shouts to quit.

We draw from her grit every day—

In the long hours where no one notices our work.

In the hard conversations where truth must be spoken.

In the silent struggles that no one else sees.

She didn't teach us resilience with lectures—

She taught us by living it in real time.

When finances were thin but generosity was wide.

When health was fragile but hope remained strong.

When dreams were delayed but she still dreamed anyway.

When we dig deep and keep moving—

She's there in our will.

When we hold on when it would be easier to let go—

She's there in our resolve.

When we smile through the weight of responsibility—

She's there, her legacy steadying our steps.

Grit is the fuel of unseen heroes.

We learned this by watching her rise again and again.

We learned this by seeing her love when it cost her everything.

We learned this by witnessing her show up, even when her heart was breaking.

The gift of her grit is not just survival—it's purpose.

As we fight for our dreams,

We carry her perseverance.

As we lift others who are struggling,

We honor her strength.

As we continue even when no one cheers,

We embody her spirit.

She gave us more than lessons—

She gave us endurance.

And now, every time we rise after falling,

Every time we believe when it would be easier not to,

Every time we refuse to let pain have the final word,

We wear her strength like armor.

When we finish the race marked out for us—

She's there in our endurance.

When we take the next hard step forward—

She's there in our determination.

When we carry others even while we ourselves are weary—

She's there, her grit beating strong within us.

Her fight lives in our courage.

Her resilience lives in our **persistence.**

Her legacy lives in every hard-won victory we step into.

As long as we endure,

Her strength will never die,

A living testimony that grit passed down is grit multiplied.

Chapter Reflection: The Gift of Her Grit: Endurance We Inherited

Scripture Reflection – KJV

"But he that shall endure unto the end, the same shall be saved."

— Matthew 24:13

Reflection Prompt

How has your mother or mother-figure's perseverance shaped your ability to endure hardships? In what areas of your life do you see her strength alive in you today?

Write your reflection below:

My Reflection:

Chapter 40

Her Unseen Sacrifice: The Quiet Love That Shaped Us

(What She Gave, We Now Cherish)

Sacrifice is more than giving something up.

It's more than letting go of comforts or possessions.

It's more than enduring pain without complaint.

Sacrifice is the silent, steady love that transforms us.

It's the invisible strength that molds our hearts.

It's the price paid in quiet moments that no one sees.

And her sacrifice still lives within us—not just in what she gave, but in how she gave it.

She didn't just give to us in moments of ease—

She gave in moments of lack.

She didn't just give when it was easy—

She gave when it hurt.

The weight of her sacrifice isn't a burden—it's a blessing.

It's a love that continues to bear fruit, even when we can't see the tree.

It's the quiet act of laying down her own desires for our well-being.

It's the unseen choice to give more when there's nothing left.

We carry her sacrifice in every act of service—

In the times we give, expecting nothing in return.

In the quiet ways we love those around us, asking for no applause.

In the strength we find when we choose others over ourselves.

She didn't just sacrifice for us in big ways—

She sacrificed in countless small, unnoticed moments.

When she gave up her dreams for ours.

When she carried burdens silently because no one else could.

When she shielded us from pain by taking it on herself.

When we choose to serve without seeking recognition—

She's there in our actions.

When we show up for others even when we're weary—

She's there in our hearts.

When we choose *love* over *self-preservation*—

She's there in our spirit, her sacrifice now ours to continue.

Sacrifice isn't just about *loss—it's about legacy*.

We learned this by **watching** her give with no expectation of repayment.

We learned it by seeing her heart expand beyond her own limitations.

We learned it by witnessing her love that didn't ask, ***"What's in it for me?"***

The quiet sacrifice she made shapes how we see others.

As we give of ourselves,

We carry her love forward.

As we bear burdens with grace,

We honor her sacrifice.

As we make choices for others over ourselves,

We live out her legacy.

She gave us more than gifts—

She gave us a model for love.

And now, every time we choose sacrifice over comfort,

Every time we put others before ourselves,

Every time we carry burdens without complaint,

We walk in the love she poured into us.

When we **love** without limits—

She's there in our hearts.

When we give without counting the cost—

She's there in our actions.

When we lay down our will for the sake of others—

She's there, her sacrifice living on in us.

Her love lives in our giving.

Her strength lives in our service.

Her legacy lives in every act of unseen sacrifice we now make.

As long as we give,

Her sacrifice will never fade,

A living testament to the love that gives without end.

Chapter Reflection: Her Unseen Sacrifice: The Quiet Love That Shaped Us

Scripture Reflection – KJV

"Greater love hath no man than this, that a man lay down his life for his friends."

— John 15:13

Reflection Prompt

In what ways has your mother or mother-figure's sacrifice shaped how you love and serve others? How do you see her example in your daily choices?

Write your reflection below:

My Reflection:

Chapter 41

The Gift of Her Laughter: Joy That Transcends Time

Laughter is more than a sound.

It's more than a reaction to something funny.

It's more than a momentary burst of joy.

Laughter is resilience in disguise.

It's a spark that ignites the soul,

A light that refuses to be dimmed.

And her laughter still echoes—not just in our memories, but in our spirits.

She didn't just laugh at jokes—

She laughed in the face of hardship.

She didn't just laugh in good times—

She laughed through tears and trials.

The gift of her laughter is not fleeting—it's eternal.

It lingers in our hearts long after the **moment** passes.

It lifts us when we're down.

It reminds us that joy is not tied to circumstances—*it's a choice.*

We hear her laughter in our *celebrations*—

In the moments we gather with loved ones.

In the light-hearted conversations that bring healing.

In the *spontaneous* giggles that fill a room with warmth.

She didn't just laugh out of habit—

She laughed because she understood the power of joy.

She laughed because she knew that laughter heals,

That it makes burdens *lighter,*

That it renews our spirits when they grow weary.

When we smile through pain—

She's there in our joy.

When we laugh even when life isn't easy—

She's there in our *resilience.*

When we choose to find humor in the smallest moments—

She's there, teaching us that laughter is the antidote to fear.

Laughter is the song of the soul.

We learned this from her carefree spirit.

We learned it in her ability to find lightness in heavy moments.

We learned it in the way she brought warmth to even the coldest days.

The gift of her laughter is a legacy we carry forward.

As we face challenges,

We choose *joy* as she did.

As we walk through life,

We celebrate the gift of humor in every moment.

As we *love* with all our hearts,

We laugh with the same freedom she taught us.

She gave us more than *joy*—

She gave us the courage to laugh in the face of adversity.

And now, every time we laugh when it would be easier to cry,

Every time we choose joy over despair,

Every time we share a moment of *lightheartedness* with others,

We honor her gift.

When we laugh with others instead of at them—

She's there in our *compassion.*

When we create space for humor even in the darkest times—

She's there in our resilience.

When we spread joy, knowing it's a choice, not a circumstance—

She's there, her laughter living on in ours.

Her joy lives in our hearts.

Her lightness lives in our spirit.

Her laughter lives in every *smile* we share.

As long as we laugh,

Her joy will never fade,

A living testimony that laughter, like love, lasts forever.

The Power of Her Presence

Chapter Reflection: The Gift of Her Laughter: Joy That Transcends Time

Scripture Reflection – KJV

"A merry heart doeth good like a medicine: but a broken spirit drieth the bones."

— Proverbs 17:22

Reflection Prompt

How has your mother or mother-figure's joy and laughter influenced your ability to find light in tough situations? In what ways do you carry her sense of humor and joy forward in your own life?

Write your reflection below:

My Reflection:

Chapter 42

The Strength of Her Silence: Lessons in Quiet Power

Silence is more than stillness.

It's more than empty space or unspoken words.

It's more than a pause in a conversation.

Silence is power.

It's the strength to endure without complaining.

It's the courage to remain calm in chaos.

It's the wisdom to know when words aren't needed.

And her silence still speaks—not just in what she refrained from saying, but in how she lived.

She didn't just hold her tongue—

She taught us that silence can be louder than any voice.

She didn't just remain quiet—

She showed us the value of listening deeply.

The strength of her silence isn't weak—it's *profound*.

It's a presence that fills the room without uttering a sound.

It's a peace that calms even the most tumultuous hearts.

It's a quiet dignity that demands respect without needing to shout.

We feel her strength in our quiet moments—

In the times when we choose to listen rather than speak.

In the peace that settles over us when chaos threatens to overtake.

In the stillness we hold when decisions must be made, not hastily, but with care.

She didn't just teach us to be silent—

She taught us to be still.

When the world demanded attention,

She knew when to pull away and reflect.

When anger threatened to rise,

She knew when to be silent and let the *storm* pass.

When we choose peace instead of conflict—

She's there in our quiet strength.

When we hold space for others' emotions—

She's there in our silence.

When we choose restraint over rash words—

She's there, her wisdom in our actions.

Silence isn't just the absence of sound—it's the presence of strength.

We learned this from her calm in the face of storms.

We learned this from her quiet confidence that didn't need to be proven.

We learned this from her ability to stand firm without ever raising her voice.

The strength of her *silence* still guides us.

As we navigate relationships,

We carry her quiet understanding.

As we *handle* conflict,

We draw from her peaceful resolve.

As we lead with gentleness,

We reflect her silent **power.**

She gave us more than words—

She gave us space to breathe.

And now, every time we listen before speaking,

Every time we choose to be present without dominating,

Every time we remain calm when others lose control,

We honor her strength.

When we pause before reacting—

She's there in our **patience.**

When we give others the space they need to speak—

She's there in our restraint.

When we move through life with quiet dignity—

She's there, her silent strength shaping our own.

Her quietness lives in our peace.

Her restraint lives in our wisdom.

Her power lives in every quiet choice we make.

As long as we listen,

Her silence will never fade,

A living testament that true power doesn't always speak.

Chapter Reflection: The Strength of Her Silence: Lessons in Quiet Power

Scripture Reflection – KJV

"Be still, and know that I am God."

— Psalm 46:10

Reflection Prompt

How did your mother or mother-figure demonstrate strength through silence? In what areas of your life do you now carry the power of quiet moments and thoughtful restraint?

Write your reflection below:

My Reflection:

Chapter 43

Her Hands of Service: A Life That Gave Without Counting

(What She Gave, We Now Offer)

Service is more than a duty.

It's more than a task checked off a list.

It's more than an obligation to fulfill.

Service is love in action.

It's the quiet giving that expects no return.

It's the steady hand that reaches out even when it's weary.

And her hands of service still move—not just in our past, but in our daily lives.

She didn't just serve when it was convenient—

She served when it was needed.

She didn't just give what was easy—

She gave what cost her most.

The gift of her service is not shallow—it's deep.

It flows in the small, unnoticed moments.

It sustains in times of exhaustion.

It brings light to the darkest places.

We live by her example every day—

In the quiet ways we serve those around us.

In the unnoticed acts of kindness that make someone else's day.

In the sacrifices we make, even when we don't have enough left for ourselves.

She didn't just serve because she was asked—

She served because it was who she was.

When there was hunger,

She made a meal.

When there was a need,

She gave what she had.

When there was a heavy heart,

She offered a listening ear.

When we serve with love, even when it's hard—

She's there in our hands.

When we give without expecting—

She's there in our hearts.

When we extend grace, even to those who may never say thank you—

She's there in our spirit, her legacy living in the service we give.

Service isn't about recognition—it's about transformation.

We learned this from her, the way she gave without seeking a reward.

We learned this from her, how she made others feel seen, heard, and loved.

We learned this from her, that the true value of service isn't in the praise—it's in the difference made.

The gift of her service is not just an example—it's a calling.

As we meet needs in the world around us,

We continue the work she began.

As we offer our time, our hearts, and our hands,

We honor her legacy of selfless giving.

As we serve others with humility,

We carry her love forward.

She gave us more than charity—

She gave us purpose.

And now, every time we put someone else before ourselves,

Every time we serve with joy instead of burden,

Every time we give out of our abundance or scarcity,

We fulfill her mission.

When we lend a hand when it's inconvenient—

She's there in our compassion.

When we give generously, even when we don't have much—

She's there in our sacrifice.

When we meet the needs of others with open hearts—

She's there, her hands still at work through ours.

Her service lives in our kindness.

Her generosity lives in our giving.

Her love lives in every act of service we offer.

As long as we serve,

Her hands will never stop moving,

A living testimony of a life that gave without counting.

Chapter Reflection: Her Hands of Service: A Life That Gave Without Counting

Scripture Reflection – KJV

"Let nothing be done through strife or vainglory; but in lowliness of mind let each esteem other better than themselves."

— Philippians 2:3

Reflection Prompt

In what ways have you been shaped by the service your mother or mother-figure gave to others? How does her example of selfless giving live on in your own actions today?

Write your reflection below:

My Reflection:

Chapter 44

The Courage of Her Voice: Speaking Truth with Grace

Courage is more than a loud proclamation.

It's more than standing in front of crowds.

It's more than shouting for attention or approval.

Courage is speaking truth, even when silence feels safer.

It's standing tall in the face of fear,

Choosing words that heal,

Speaking the heart even when it's hard.

Her courage wasn't just in her actions—it was in her voice.

She didn't just speak for herself—

She spoke for the voiceless.

She didn't just speak for change—

She spoke for understanding.

The courage of her voice isn't forgotten—it lives on.

It echoes in the conversations we begin.

It strengthens us when our words seem inadequate.

It calls us to rise, even when the world tries to silence us.

We hear her voice every day—

In the moments we speak up when it's uncomfortable.

In the courage to stand by what's right, even if we stand alone.

In the strength to be truthful, even when truth brings pain.

She didn't just speak her truth—

She helped us find ours.

When society was quick to judge,

She taught us to listen.

When fear tried to silence us,

She taught us to speak louder, with compassion.

When we stand for justice,

She's there in our boldness.

When we call out injustice,

She's there in our resolve.

When we speak love in the face of hate,

She's there in our courage.

Courage doesn't always roar—it sometimes whispers.

We learned this from her quiet strength.

We learned it from the way she handled difficult conversations with grace.

We learned it from the way she held truth in one hand and love in the other.

The courage of her voice still resounds.

As we fight for what's right,

We carry her fearless speech.

As we speak out for others who have no voice,

We walk in her footsteps.

As we tell stories of justice and hope,

We are living her legacy.

She gave us more than words—

She gave us conviction.

And now, every time we use our voice to protect,

Every time we speak truth over lies,

Every time we stand firm in love and justice,

We honor her courage.

When we speak with confidence,

She's there in our certainty.

When we speak for those who cannot speak,

She's there in our compassion.

When we speak truth in love, even at a cost,

She's there, her courage breathing life into ours.

Her voice lives in our advocacy.

Her truth lives in our convictions.

Her grace lives in every word we now speak.

As long as we speak,

Her courage will never fade,

A living reminder that truth spoken with love has the power to change everything.

Chapter Reflection: The Courage of Her Voice: Speaking Truth with Grace

Scripture Reflection – KJV

"Thou art my hiding place and my shield: I hope in thy word."

— Psalm 119:114

Reflection Prompt

How has your mother or mother-figure's courage to speak truth shaped your ability to stand firm in your own beliefs? In what areas of your life do you find her voice still guiding your choices and actions?

Write your reflection below:

My Reflection:

Chapter 45

Her Quiet Strength: Power in Stillness

Strength is more than loud declarations.

It's more than the force of a raised voice or the flash of a bold action.

It's more than muscle or might in the open.

Strength is stillness.

It's the ability to stand firm without making a sound.

It's the courage to endure in silence.

And her strength still echoes—not just in the actions she took, but in the quiet power she displayed.

She didn't demand attention—

She earned respect with her presence.

She didn't shout for recognition—

She built a legacy that spoke for itself.

The power of her quiet strength isn't easily seen—it's felt.

It's the calm that fills the room when she enters.

It's the confidence that never wavers, even when the world tries to knock it down.

It's the steadiness that others rely on when everything else seems unstable.

We feel her **quie**t strength every day—

In the moments we remain patient when impatience calls.

In the times we choose peace when conflict could be easier.

In the days when we walk through challenges, undeterred and unwavering.

She didn't teach us strength by fighting battles—

She taught us strength by enduring them with grace.

When everything was against her,

She stood tall.

When the pressure mounted,

She didn't break.

When the world expected her to fold,

She remained unshaken.

When we pause to take a breath before reacting—

She's there in our composure.

When we choose silence over argument—

She's there in our wisdom.

When we carry a burden without complaining—

She's there in our perseverance.

Strength doesn't always have to roar—

Sometimes it speaks in the quiet moments of resolve.

We learned this from her ability to remain firm when everything around her crumbled.

We learned this from her quiet example, unspoken yet loud in its impact.

The power of her stillness doesn't retreat—it resounds.

As we face life's storms,

We stand firm on the foundation she laid.

As we navigate relationships,

We lead with calm rather than chaos.

As we make decisions,

We remember that sometimes the strongest thing to do is wait and trust.

She gave us more than answers—

She gave us presence.

And now, every time we remain calm in the chaos,

Every time we refuse to let circumstances dictate our peace,

Every time we endure hardship without complaint,

We reflect her quiet strength.

When we choose silence in a heated moment—

She's there in our discipline.

When we face uncertainty with resolve—

She's there in our conviction.

When we walk through life's challenges without losing our peace—

She's there, her strength silently guiding us.

Her calm lives in our poise.

Her fortitude lives in our persistence.

Her power lives in every quiet moment of determination.

As long as we stand still in the storm,

Her quiet strength will never fade,

A living testament that the greatest power often lies in stillness.

Chapter Reflection: Her Quiet Strength: Power in Stillness

Scripture Reflection – KJV

"But the Lord is in his holy temple: let all the earth keep silence before him."

— Habakkuk 2:20

Reflection Prompt

In what ways has your mother or mother-figure's quiet strength shaped the way you handle challenges? How does her example of stillness influence your approach to difficult situations?

Write your reflection below:

My Reflection:

Chapter 46

The Bridge of Her Presence: Connecting Hearts Across Time

(What She Built, We Now Cross)

Presence is more than being in the same room.

It's more than a body sitting at the table.

It's more than a voice filling the silence.

Presence is connection.

It's a thread that links hearts beyond distance.

It's a foundation that holds us steady, even when we're apart.

And her presence still connects us—not just in space, but in spirit.

She didn't just occupy a place—

She made it sacred.

She didn't just show up—

She showed up with love, with purpose, with intention.

The bridge of her presence is not fleeting—it's eternal.

It spans across time and distance.

It connects us in our highest joys and our deepest sorrows.

It holds us together when life threatens to pull us apart.

We feel her presence every day—

In the memories that live in our hearts.

In the lessons she taught without speaking.

In the quiet strength that echoes in moments of uncertainty.

She didn't just touch our lives—

She transformed them.

When her hands held us close,

When her eyes saw us for who we really were,

When her words spoke truth into our souls,

She was building something that would last long after she was gone.

When we laugh with joy,

She's there in the smile we carry.

When we grieve with sorrow,

She's there in the comfort she once gave.

When we choose love over division,

She's there, the bridge she built connecting us to what truly matters.

Her presence is not limited by time or space.

It stretches across the years,

Across the miles,

Across the silence that sometimes separates us from those we love.

The bridge of her presence still holds strong.

As we walk through life,

We cross it every day.

As we reach out to others,

We extend the same love she poured into us.

As we hold one another,

We honor the connection she first made.

She gave us more than a memory—

She gave us a way to be together, forever.

And now, every time we show up for someone else,

Every time we stay present even when it's hard,

Every time we bridge gaps with love and patience,

We walk the path she laid.

When we build our own bridges with grace—

She's there in the strength of the structure.

When we stand firm, no matter what the distance—

She's there in the foundation.

When we build communities of connection and support—

She's there, her presence continuing to bind us all.

Her legacy lives in our connection to one another.

Her love lives in the bridges we now build.

Her spirit lives in every heart we touch with kindness.

As long as we live,

Her presence will never fade,

A living testament to the power of love that binds us across time and space.

Chapter Reflection: The Bridge of Her Presence: Connecting Hearts Across Time

Scripture Reflection – KJV

"Where two or three are gathered together in my name, there am I in the midst of them."

— Matthew 18:20

Reflection Prompt

How has your mother or mother-figure's presence impacted your life? In what ways do you continue to feel connected to her, even in her absence?

Write your reflection below:

My Reflection:

Chapter 30

We're Still Becoming Her Legacy

(This Is Not the End—It's the Continuation)

They say when someone passes, you're supposed to find closure.

But when it comes to her…

There is no closing.

No finish line to what she started.

Because what she built in us continues to evolve, stretch, and shape our lives in ways we're still discovering.

We're not just carrying her memory—

We're becoming her legacy.

That legacy didn't end the day she took her last breath.

It lives in the way we breathe through hard days now.

It lives in the way we speak up for what's right,
hold space for others, and love with the kind of depth only
she could have taught.

We are still growing into the men she raised us to be.

Still learning how to love without limits.

Still learning how to lead with patience.

Still learning how to listen before we speak, how to give without strings, how to endure with joy even when life tests our strength.

We're still learning how to be brave—

Not in loud, flashy ways, but in the quiet, faithful ways she showed us.

She didn't teach us through lectures—

She taught us through living.

Her legacy isn't locked in the past.

It's woven into the present.

It speaks in our tone, shows up in our choices, and echoes in how we care for others.

Every time we resist the urge to give up—

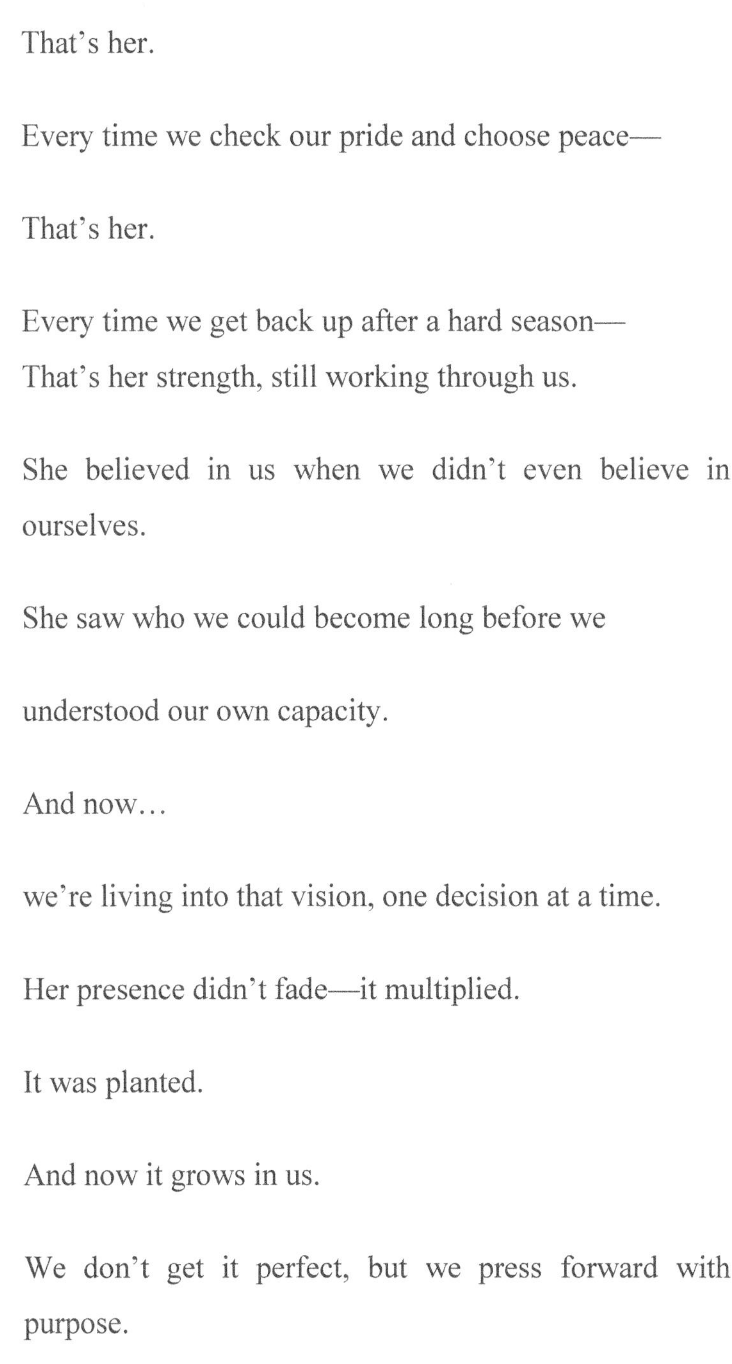

That's her.

Every time we check our pride and choose peace—

That's her.

Every time we get back up after a hard season—
That's her strength, still working through us.

She believed in us when we didn't even believe in ourselves.

She saw who we could become long before we

understood our own capacity.

And now…

we're living into that vision, one decision at a time.

Her presence didn't fade—it multiplied.

It was planted.

And now it grows in us.

We don't get it perfect, but we press forward with purpose.

We're not trying to replace her—we could never.

But what we can do is **reflect** her.

Represent her.

Rebuild the world she dreamed of—one marked by faith, decency, and love.

We are her fruit.

We are her reflection.

We are her voice now in rooms she'll never enter.

Her hands extended in places she'll never touch.

Her heart beating through the lives we impact.

And when we miss her—and we will—

We remember that missing her is part of carrying her.

It means she mattered.

It means she still matters.

It means we are still walking in the direction she pointed us toward.

This isn't the conclusion of her story—

It's the continuation.

Because legacies don't end.

They **expand**.

They grow.

They deepen.

We are becoming that legacy—

Every time we forgive.

Every time we uplift someone.

Every time we pass along the wisdom she gave us without fanfare.

We are still becoming…

Still evolving…

Still honoring her…

And that's how she lives on.

Not just through memories—

But through motion.

Not just in photos—

But in people.

Not just through what she did—

But through **who we're still becoming.**

Chapter Reflection: We're Still Becoming Her Legacy

Scripture Reflection – KJV

"And let us not be weary in well doing: for in due season we shall reap, if we faint not."
— *Galatians 6:9*

Reflection Prompt

In what ways do you feel yourself becoming the legacy your mother left behind? How do your actions, values, and relationships reflect the foundation she laid—and how can you honor her daily through the life you continue to build?

Write your reflection below:

My Reflection

Prayer of Gratitude

(For Her Life, Her Love, Her Legacy)

Heavenly Father,

Thank You for the gift of her presence.

Thank You for the life she lived, the love she gave, and the lessons she instilled.

Even in her absence, we feel her near—guiding, comforting, and shaping our steps.

Thank You for the strength she carried quietly,
for the sacrifices she made that we didn't always see,
and for the prayers she whispered that still cover us today.

Thank You for her hands that worked, her heart that nurtured, and her faith that anchored our family.

Thank You for her laughter, her discipline, her encouragement, and her unwavering belief in us.

We are who we are because You placed her in our lives.

Lord, help us to honor her not only in memory, but in movement.

Help us to live out her values, to love like she did, and to lead with the same grace she modeled.

Give us the strength to keep becoming what she hoped for—
To carry her legacy with humility, with integrity, and with joy.

And for those whose hearts still ache with loss,
bring comfort, healing, and holy reminders that she is never truly gone—

because what she gave us lives on.

Thank You, Lord, for her presence in our past, her imprint on our present, and her influence over our future.

We bless Your name for the precious gift of a mother.
May her life be a light that leads us closer to You.

In Jesus' name we pray,

Amen.

Final Letter to the Reader

(From One Heart to Another)

Dear Reader,

Thank you.

Thank you for taking this journey through love, loss, memory, and legacy.

Thank you for sitting at this table with me—page after page—where the presence of a mother still lingers, still leads, and still lives.

Whether you are grieving your mother, honoring her, or learning to appreciate her in new ways, I want you to know this:

You are not alone.

If you've ever felt the sting of her absence…
If you've ever smiled through tears at a memory only you hold…

If you've ever caught yourself doing something and thought, *"That's exactly what she would've done…"*
That's her presence.

Still working.

Still comforting.

Still shaping you.

The truth is, a mother's influence doesn't end with goodbye.

Her love doesn't expire.

Her values don't disappear.

Her prayers don't stop working.

She lives on—in you.

In how you love.

In how you serve.

In how you rise each day with her strength stitched into your soul.

You are her continuation.

And if this book reminded you of the beauty of her sacrifices, the depth of her guidance, and the power of her love, then honor her in the most profound way possible:

Live it forward.

Pass it on to your children, your family, your community.

Be the arms someone else needs.

Be the voice of encouragement.

Be the calm in someone else's storm.

Be the reflection of the one who poured so much into you.

If your mother is still with you—hold her closer.

Ask more questions.

Watch her wisdom in motion.

Cherish every second.

And if your mother has passed on,

Know that what she left within you is enough to keep growing, enough to keep giving, enough to light the way for someone else.

You are her legacy now.

So keep becoming.

Keep building.

Keep loving.

And always remember—

Her presence is not just a memory.

It's your movement.

It's your mission.

It's your strength.

It's your story.

With gratitude and grace,

Ethan L. Ketterer

Author of The Power of Her Presence

A Space for Your Thoughts

(Use these pages to reflect, remember, and release)

Sometimes there are thoughts that don't fit neatly into a chapter.

Moments that rise unexpectedly.

Feelings too big for a prompt, but too sacred to forget.

These pages are for those moments.

Write freely.

Write honestly.

Write as if she's listening—because maybe, in some way, she still is.

Your Thoughts

A Letter to Her

What I Wish I Could Say One More Time

A Memory I'll Never Forget